TAKE

A

WALK

ON

THE

NARC

SIDE

DEDICATION

This book is dedicated to four amazing human beings.

The first is someone who inspires me every single day and offers me unconditional, authentic love. She has been my constant support and best friend my entire life. There are no words adequate enough to describe how incredibly grateful and proud I am that I get to call her *Mum*.

The second is someone who came into my life unexpectedly, at a time when I had very little reason to smile. He restored my faith in genuine love, in trust, in commitment and stood by me through some of the darkest days I have ever had to endure. He has wiped my tears, held my hand and been my teammate throughout every challenge. He is my heart, my home, my friend, my love…he is my *Mr*.

Not only did you both nurture my idea of writing this book, but together you offered me continual encouragement and unwavering support to enable me to make this dream come true.

Last, but not least, I would like to mention my two beautiful, talented and highly sarcastic daughters Tia and Brooke, without whom this book would have been completed a lot sooner!! I hope you both find true and honest love with someone who has compassion, empathy and honour. May your heart always be happy xx

INDEX

INTRODUCTION

For those of you picking up this book who have had first-hand experience of dealing with a narcissistic individual, I can undoubtedly say you look back over that period of your life with regret, unimaginable hurt and quite often unresolved confusion. I know this because I've been there too.

We are all only too aware that identifying these profoundly immoral and quite frankly warped human beings is not as straightforward as one might imagine. Narcissists aren't known for dressing in red and white striped jumpers with matching bobble hats…if only it was as simple as finding Wally!

In an ideal world life would be much easier if all the dangerous, deluded and borderline insane individuals identified themselves upfront. Perhaps they could even wear some sort of badge displaying a public health and safety warning. If only that were the case, then much less harm would be done to those of us who may otherwise fall victim to their cruel mentality. In another world maybe, but not this one I'm sorry to say.

However, that said, I do hope this book brings you some comfort in its relatability to your regrettable experience and that you can resonate with the stories told and find solace in the knowledge you are not alone.

For those of you picking up this book who have not yet fallen foul to or suffered at the hands of one of these delusional, egocentric, cruel, selfish, deceitful, manipulative and coercive individuals and wish to educate yourself, so that you may avoid the trauma they create - well done you! This book is going to be your resource tool and will hopefully empower you with the knowledge and awareness needed to spot the red flags as you take **A Walk on the Narc Side** through the experiences of those who have unfortunately fallen victim and paid the price.

The stories you are about to read are true.

Names and places have been changed to protect the identity of the victims.

CHAPTER 1

WHAT ARE WE DEALING WITH?

While the concept of narcissism was first identified as a mental disorder in 1898 by the British essayist and physician Havelock Ellis, it's only really been in the last 50 years that narcissistic personality disorder has become recognised as a mental illness. It was officially recognised in the third edition of the Diagnostic and Statistical Manual of Mental Disorder in 1980.

Many years have passed since that official recognition in 1980 and even though the words 'Narcissist' or 'Narcissism' have been around for a very long time, it would appear they have only recently become common in modern day language. However, although these words can often be batted around in conversations, we still seem to have very little understanding of Narcissistic abuse and it remains one of the least talked about forms of abuse in modern day society. It saddens me to write that the brazen predators and their helpless victims tend to go unnoticed, which is testament to our lack of awareness. Why is it that we seem to have so little understanding about this insidious form of abuse?

Unfortunately, the answer lies in the nature of the beast. Narcissistic abuse is subtle, it often catches the victim off guard while it exploits their emotional vulnerabilities and natural empathy. A Narcissist uses various tactics such as control and manipulation to deepen the victim's dependency on them, weakening their confidence and creating an environment of confusion and heartache. This psychological entrapment can go on for years and years before their victim realises what's going on, with many never being able to fully escape from it.

For family, friends and even work colleagues of the victims there are often no signs, no physical appearance of abuse and, given that every victim has an empathetic personality, they tend to make excuses for their abuser. They may cover things up or deny things that are happening in an innocent attempt to protect themselves and their abuser.

Many victims unfortunately display misplaced loyalty and compassion to the point that they even try to find ways to 'help' or 'fix' their abuser, doing so because they truly believe them to be a good person underneath it all. All of which are completely futile. Trying to change a narcissist is like trying to eat soup with a fork: an utterly pointless, frustrating and time-consuming task.

Victims of narcissistic abuse often become desensitised to reality and their drastically changed lifestyle becomes 'normal'. Slowly over time they are oppressed by their perpetrator and the person they had once been gradually disappears making way for a new, conditioned version of themselves to appear. They begin to accept the perilous treatment they endure with a 'get up and get on with things' attitude, ignorant to the fact that they are victims of an insidiously cruel and systematic form of psychological abuse.

Sadly, this is the reason why narcissistic abuse is taking so long to break through the channels of education and awareness in society; the victims simply do not realise they are victims due to the insidious way that the narcissistic abuse has changed them and indeed their perception of themselves. What's often worse is that even in situations where the victim does become aware of it, many are too afraid to speak out and expose their abuser. Although they may have escaped from the abusive relationship, the perpetrator is often still able to inflict their dominance, control and manipulation upon them. This is especially true if they share children together.

It's sad to say, as a fellow survivor of narcissist abuse, I hold my hands up to it - we protect them out of equal measures of love and fear and in turn we unmindfully enable them. Obviously, this is not something we do intentionally, but that is one of the most dangerous parts of narcissistic abuse; their ability to slowly, over time, break you down into someone who conforms and accepts their treatment. This can even be the case after you have escaped the relationship and come to understand that their treatment was wrong and abusive. We still often stay silent. This may be due to fear of consequences from the narc, it could be because we feel embarrassment or shame at having allowed ourselves to become victim to such a hideous individual, or simply because we want to just forget about the whole thing, lock it up in the past and move forward as we attempt to rebuild our lives.

My conclusion, in a nutshell, as to why narcissistic abuse remains one of the most prolific and hidden forms of abuse is because the victims who suffer at the hands of narcissists don't speak up and sadly those who do often aren't believed. The narc is a master of manipulation and is primed and ready to take on the lead role as the victim in any story which might risk their exposure. Often those victims who are brave enough to attempt to tell their side of the story are sadly bullied, harassed and ultimately forced into submission by the narc, paving the way for other victims in similar situations to stay silent.

That might sound like a very simple conclusion, but without the resilient bravery and strength of the victim, without their voice, without their willingness to share their experiences with others how can we, as a society, be equipped to recognise a narcissistic individual?

This of course is not the fault of the victim in any shape or form. They have been subjected to a cruel and deliberate trauma at the hands of an abuser and each of those victims will deal with that trauma in the best way they know how. I empathise with those who feel the need to lock it up and put their horrendous and often life changing experiences firmly in the past. I also understand their desire to stay quiet for fear of repercussions and harassment from the narc.

As a survivor of narcissistic abuse myself, as someone who managed to withstand over 14 years of psychological manipulation and control, I am forever thankful that I was able to overcome my loss of self-identity, self-esteem, severe anxiety and financial ruin. By establishing the No Contact Rule I am now narc free. By setting boundaries to protect my mental health and educate myself on the impacts of narcissistic abuse, I have been able to heal and rediscover who I really am.

It is because of my personal and often challenging journey that I am inspired to help others. I feel compelled to create much needed awareness and understanding around the topic of narcissism, the insidious way it plays out in relationships and the life changing impacts it can have on victims. Together we can hopefully prevent many more individuals falling victim to this horrendous form of psychological abuse.

What you are about to read will hopefully take you on a journey of newfound awareness of narcissistic abuse. I hope it will become a resource tool not only for yourself but for your children, your sisters, your brothers, your friends, your parents - because narcissist abuse has no bearing on your age, sex or status in this world. Any one of us can fall victim to these masters of emotional manipulation.

I, along with every other victim whose stories you are about to read, only wished there had been a book like this when we were growing up. Maybe then our choices would have been very different.

CHAPTER 2

RED FLAGS

When we talk about narcissism, we are either referring to the personality disorder known as NPD which is a recognised mental health condition, or we can be talking about an individual who displays narcissistic traits.

So, what's the difference? Well, in short you will meet many people throughout your lifetime from different walks of life who display narcissistic traits and each one of these individuals will display those traits on various levels. In contrast, you will probably never in your lifetime meet someone who has been clinically diagnosed with NPD. The reason for this is due to the very nature of the disorder which gives the individual an overrated sense of self-importance, arrogance and the belief that they are superior to everyone else. These people therefore see themselves as perfect and are unable to possess the insight and self-awareness to accept that they may have NPD and so seeking a medical diagnosis is something they are never going to consider doing.

In today's modern world, narcissistic traits are more common in society than ever before – possibly one of the saddest reflections of the ever-changing world we live in. There are various factors which have contributed to the rise of individuals displaying these traits, with social media influences being top of the list. There have been multiple studies carried out over recent years which have found a strong link between social media usage and the increase in narcissistic traits being displayed in young people.

This is not to say that using social media will necessarily make someone a narcissist, but it does highlight the fact that it's a place used by many people who display high levels of narcissistic traits. Therefore, it is entirely understandable that these traits can be learnt or copied by their audiences, especially those who have young, impressionable minds.

Social media is used by the *grandiose narcissist* as it provides an easily accessible way to obtain admiration and praise from thousands of people across the entire world. Using it as an outlet to express their over-inflated sense of self, the grandiose narcissist achieves great satisfaction as their attention-seeking posts and selfies gain them more and more likes, shares and followers from an audience who are ultimately being utilized to stroke their narcissistic egos.

Social media is also used as a tool by the *vulnerable narcissist* who tends to have low emotional stability, or the *victim narcissist* who always has a 'poor me' story to tell. With the use of social media, these individuals can create the self-image they desire, manipulating their audience into plying them with sympathy and support which they may not receive in the real world.

Before reading through the following **Red Flags** it is important to note that an individual who occasionally displays one or more of the following narcissistic traits does not automatically fall into the category of being a full-blown narcissist, nor does it mean they have NPD as I mentioned at the beginning of this book. However, a person who is displaying one or more of these traits on a regular basis without concern or consideration for others, would be someone you should avoid like the Bubonic plague!

Narcissistic traits include:

*Overrated sense of self-importance

*Never admitting fault

*Entitled

*Manipulative

*May have a charming and charismatic character

*Abusive

*Exploit others for their own gain

*Lack of empathy

*Dishonest

*Shifts blame onto others

*Envious of others

*Quick to anger

*Volatile

*Unfaithful

*Attention seeking

*An unfair and unjust need for power and control

*Dismissive of the feelings of others

*Needs admiration

*Greed

*Selfishness

Unfortunately, this is not an exhaustive list. However these are the most commonly displayed traits we need to watch out for. Hopefully, with more understanding and awareness we can all learn to identify them as red flags long before we fall victim to them.

Now, I'm sure many of you reading this will be able to identify not just one individual in your life, but probably several people who display at least one of these traits – so does that make them a narcissist? No. What about if they display three or four of these traits, does that make them a narcissist? Not necessarily.

It is the level to which the traits are displayed, the repeated pattern of behaviours and most importantly the lack of empathy the individual holds that makes them a narcissistic individual.

If someone tells a lie for example, admits to their wrongdoing, apologises and does not repeat the same behaviour again then they cannot be classed as a narcissistic individual even though dishonesty is a narcissistic trait. The individual has taken responsibility, made a genuine apology and learnt from their mistake – not repeating the same behaviour again.

However, if someone tells a lie and refuses to take responsibility, shifts the blame onto someone else, doesn't apologise or perhaps apologises in a half-hearted way, that's an indication of a red flag. If they continue to repeat the same behaviours regardless of the hurt it causes others, refusing to respect the boundaries, showing no remorse or empathy, then this is an example of someone who shows high levels of narcissistic traits and can be classed as a narcissistic individual.

It's important to note that narcissistic traits can be present in anyone. They can be displayed by a family member, a friend or work colleague but what is possibly the most controlling and life destroying situation is when the narcissist is your partner. The reason why I say this is because when the narcissist is a friend, work colleagues or a family member, there are options for you to remove the toxic individual from your life or at the very least minimise contact or communication with them. This may mean leaving a friend group, getting a transfer at work or speaking to a senior member of staff about taking on a different role within the organisation to minimise contact with a narcissistic colleague, or even cutting ties with family members. However, when the narcissist is your wife or husband, girlfriend or boyfriend and particularly if you have kids together it's a very different situation. The connecting elements of a relationship whether that be a joint mortgage, shared debt or property, family commitments, etc. all become a twisted web which gives the narcissist a much stronger hold over you, and your options to leave or distance yourself from the narc become very limited.

Enduring and ending a relationship with a narcissist is without doubt one of the most challenging experiences anyone will ever have to go through. It takes bravery and strength to free yourself from their control and manipulation. It takes remarkable resilience to withstand the post separation abuse, not to mention the emotional turbulence you will inevitably go through as you attempt to process the trauma you have suffered at their hands. Unfortunately, it doesn't end there. Once you have found your freedom from the narc, you must establish a positive mindset and learn to develop a level of patience and confidence as you learn to love and value yourself all over again. This is imperative in order to fully heal from the trauma and restore your life, as you are about to learn through the stories of those who suffered and survived.

CHAPTER 3

ONCE UPON A TIME

When you first become involved in a romantic relationship with a narcissist, you will be forgiven for experiencing feelings of pure exhilaration that feel so electrifying they are almost beyond words. Almost instantly there appears to be an intense connection between you both and this newfound love resonates with you like nothing you've ever experienced before. You feel as though you have been swept off your feet and transported into a whimsical world of love and romance, arousing such passion that it leaves you feeling utterly convinced you have met the man or woman of your dreams. They wrap you up in their over-the-top displays of attention, their tenderness and emotional declarations of flattery, praise and love to such a degree that you genuinely feel you have met your soulmate, your kindred spirit, your happy ever after.

However, all is not what it seems I'm sorry to say, and the butterflies you feel in your stomach are not caused by genuine love, at least not on their part anyway. These feelings are simply the result of a very influential tactic the

narc possesses within their arsenal which is referred to as
Love Bombing.

As humans, we are wired to seek love, companionship, connection and intimacy in order to feel accepted, valued and appreciated as a person. Therefore, it is entirely understandable that when we meet someone who displays these highly desirable qualities and attributes, we can be quickly drawn to them. However, as anyone with previous experience of having a narcissistic partner will know, what you thought was your knight in shining armour insidiously turns out to be nothing more than a highly skilled manipulator with an over-inflated ego dressed in tin foil!

Before long, the romance, affection and companionship they once offered you diminishes and is replaced with devaluation, control, dishonesty, selfishness, intimidation, gaslighting and in many cases infidelity.

Your ability to recognise this change in behaviour can often be somewhat clouded as you attempt to grasp onto the person they once were at the beginning of the relationship. You accept that all relationships have their ups and downs and so convince yourself that these issues will get resolved and things will return to normal. The sad thing about all this is that *normal* never actually was normal. What you believed this person to be at the beginning of the relationship was just an act. A selfish and deliberate act carried out by a narcissistic individual to gain your trust, loyalty, admiration and emotional attachment. Once the narc determines that they have achieved their self-serving goal and they have successfully secured you as their supply everything changes, and before you know it you have become their prisoner.

'ALISON'

<u>MISPLACED LOYALTY</u>

I wouldn't exactly call my first encounter with Ray love-at-first sight. I don't recall experiencing those often talked about feelings of butterflies or childish excitement. He was just an ordinary guy, a friend of a friend who happened to be in the same pub at the same time as me. Apart from our brief introduction and a friendly nod in each other's direction to acknowledge one another, there had been no mutual attraction or interest shown. There weren't any long, lingering looks at each other across the table, or getting-to-know-you chit chat. There wasn't even an offer to buy me a drink. For all intents and purposes, that evening was just like any other. That was of course until I was leaving. I had said my goodbyes to the group and just as I was searching through my handbag for my car keys at the door of the pub, Ray appeared almost out of nowhere. He caught me totally by surprise, the result of which was a word or two of profanity from me and a nervous jump which made me grab my chest as if my heart was somehow going to attempt to escape. Oh boy, if only I had known what was coming. If only I could go back in time and revisit that night in question, then I think I might be tempted to begin open heart surgery on myself right there at the entrance of the pub. I would remove my poor, innocent heart from the trauma it was about to endure at the hands of this man and replace it with a block of wood! If only!

After offering his apologies for startling me, Ray asked me if I wouldn't mind giving him a lift home as he didn't live far. Apparently, this suggestion came from our mutual friend at the table who obviously fancied herself as a bit of a cupid, having seen us both making moves to leave at the same time. I don't know what it is with some people; they know two single people and just assume they must be lonely and decide to play match maker!

I had always been quite shy and didn't seem to attract much male attention. Don't get me wrong, I was completely happy in my own company, and I wasn't hankering after a relationship. I was just happy plodding along in life. I had had a couple of short-term relationships over the years, nothing too serious…no dinners with parents or conversations about prospective baby names. Both had amicably run their course and, I suppose and just fizzled out. I was only 23 and to be honest I wasn't entirely sure I even knew what love really was. I certainly hadn't experienced anything that resembled the all-consuming type of love you see in the movies or read about in books. Then again, I was also sceptical if that kind of love even existed in real life. That was until of course that fateful night when Ray asked me to give him a lift home and he single handedly changed all that.

Suddenly - and I mean suddenly, I seemed to take all leave of my senses and within that short 20-minute drive from the pub to Ray's house I seemed to evolve into a love-struck, giggling, excited teenager. I was totally mesmerised by this man. I have no clue what magical wizardry was in play that evening, and I couldn't blame alcohol as I hadn't taken any due to the fact I was driving, but Ray was having such a powerful effect on me that when he asked me for my phone number as we arrived at his house, I gave it to him without so much as a second thought.

That night after returning home, as I lay in bed, still smiling like a cheshire cat from the effects of Ray, my phone lit up with a message. It was him. And so, it began. We spent the next four hours and thirty-six minutes in full-on text mode; fingers moving faster than a secretary on amphetamines and with each reply I received I could literally feel my fondness and affection for Ray growing. The conversation was light-hearted yet inquisitive. He was keen to learn all about me, asking real questions which inspired an openness in me that I had never experienced before. He was different from anyone I had ever met. He made me feel free, uplifted and connected to him in such a way that even now I struggle to find the words to describe it, but I remember thinking, this must be what love feels like.

Before long we were a couple. A couple very much in love with each other. We were utterly besotted and spent every spare minute we had together. There was never a cross word spoken between us and Ray honestly made me feel like I was the only person in the world. He sent adorable messages throughout the day when we were both at work telling me how much he loved me and how fate had brought us together and I couldn't help but agree with him. I was happier than I'd ever been, happier than I ever thought possible.

Both of us owned our own homes and within the first couple of months a discussion arose about moving in together. At first, I was a little taken aback by Ray's suggestion but any initial concerns I may have had about things moving too fast, were soon eradicated from my mind as Ray chatted excitedly about how great it would be to wake up beside me every morning, enjoy breakfast together and watch movies in the evenings. He made it all sound so picture perfect, and given the fairytale path we had been on for the past few months it seemed the ideal next step. Some of my family and friends offered their words of caution about moving in with someone I had only known for such a short period of time, but I brushed their concerns aside in the firm knowledge that I knew better. I knew Ray and I knew he was my soulmate. Or so I thought.

It was agreed that I would rent my property out on a long-term lease and move into Ray's house. I am not entirely sure how we came to this decision but looking back on it now, I can safely say, all decisions were greatly driven by Ray. His house was closer to his work but much further from mine, however Ray managed to persuade me to overlook this by saying he would be home first every evening and would be able to do the cooking. So, I rented my house out to a lovely family on a long-term agreement and moved myself and my belongings into Ray's.

When I tell you that the ink of my signature on the rental agreement wasn't even dry, I mean it, when everything began to change. Moving in day was full of tension and aggravation. Ray didn't see the reason for me to have wardrobe space in the main bedroom and instead insisted that I use the much smaller wardrobe in the second bedroom. He didn't seem keen on any of my personal belongings and family pictures being on display, telling me that he much more preferred the *"minimalist look"* even though there were plenty of his personal pictures and football memorabilia on show around the house.

I put the sudden shift in his mood down to stress, even though us moving in together should have been a happy occasion, I appreciated that it was a big change for him so I politely went along with his suggestions of using the smaller wardrobe and keeping my personal possessions in a box where according to Ray "they would be much safer". Unfortunately, the days that followed were not much better and Ray's crabbed and ill-tempered mood remained. He was unnecessarily irritable and distant with me and completely unwilling to engage in conversation when I broached the subject of his dramatic change in demeanour. There were some good days when he would greet me as I came through the door with a smile and a hug. However, those occasions were usually followed up by some underhanded remark about how dry my skin looked or a patronizing look as he asked me if I brushed my hair that morning. There were no romantic meals cooked for me coming home like he'd promised. There wasn't even food in the fridge most days as it appeared the task of shopping seemed to have been bestowed onto me, along with the cleaning, the cooking and the paying of the bills. Meanwhile, Ray worked, went to the gym, watched football at the weekends and was always too tired to watch a movie or go for a walk with me.

Over the next few months, I went from feeling like the most important person in Ray's life to the most insignificant being in the entire world. I felt like I had not only lost his love, respect, loyalty and attention but that I had lost me. I didn't know who I was. Where had my fun loving, independent self disappeared to? I was exhausted from trying to figure it out. Exhausted from the amount of energy I was putting into trying to 'fix' things, to somehow get our relationship back to how it used to be. I didn't understand the change in Ray any more than I understood the change in myself. I wasn't sleeping and my moods were all over the place. It was like I was living in a constant state of confusion mixed with high levels of anxiety, but still I stayed with him. I had made a commitment to him, to us and I wasn't going to turn my back on that.

Of course, as time went on, I continued in my attempts of talking to Ray about the change in his behaviours. I even challenged him on his disrespect towards me, but I was sternly shut down and told that I was being ridiculous. He would say I was being oversensitive and that I was making mountains out of mole hills. He complained about my mood swings which sparked an intense feeling of guilt within me causing me to start apologising to him on what felt like a daily basis. I was sorry that his dinner was a bit late. I was sorry that I hadn't taken the bins out because I had fallen asleep at 7pm due to pure exhaustion. I was sorry for calling him while he was watching the football. I was sorry that my hair was messy, and my makeup wasn't perfect. I was always sorry, but still I stayed.

I stayed in that soul-destroying relationship for another two years. I did think about leaving but I had nowhere to go as I had foolishly agreed to forego my own home and move into his. To be totally truthful, I was full of embarrassment and shame. Embarrassed about telling the world that I had fallen in love with someone I hardly even knew only to discover they were not who they were pretending to be at all, in fact they were the complete opposite. That loving, carefree guy who appeared infatuated by me and so openly declared his love for me was just a front. A front for the selfish, controlling, egotistic man he really was.

When I look back now, I remember how he sat quietly in the pub on the night we met, happily engaging in conversation now and again with our mutual friends. He was listening and watching. He was taking it all in. Taking me in. Somehow, within those couple of hours Ray had gathered enough information about me, worked out what sort of person I was; kind, quiet and perhaps a little naive and in his egotistical and narcissistic mentality, determined that I was someone he could easily manipulate for his own selfish needs. His next move was inevitable as he swooped in with all the charm and charisma of a fairytale prince and swept me off my feet.

Once Ray had gained control over the relationship; once he knew I was head over heels in love with him, that he had managed to persuade me (which I will admit wasn't a hard job given the fairy tale head spin he had created) to move into his house and forsake my own, he knew he had me caught. Hook, line and sinker as the saying goes. I had developed a connection with Ray, an attachment of sorts which was both psychological and emotional. I was desperately holding onto the guy I had met at the beginning of the relationship. However, in reality, I was actually holding onto a person who didn't even exist. Sadly, that bond, the connection Ray had masterfully created with me from the very first day, kept me in that toxic relationship for much longer than I should have been there.

I lost myself in that relationship. Ray had used his narcissistic love bombing techniques to expertly captivate me, to lure me in so that I would become his means of supply. Once he realised that he was in a position of power and control within the relationship, he managed to turn me into his ambiguous prisoner. I became locked in my own head where constant feelings of confusion, depression and low self-esteem were my unwelcome cell mates and for two long years Ray never once offered me the same love and attention he did so easily at the beginning. What I truly thought was my happy-ever-after-love-story was nothing more than an elaborate game of make believe made possible by a highly skilled manipulator and my own misplaced loyalty.

Thankfully, that's all in the past now but I still bear the psychological scars. They say that time heals all wounds, however I don't think that's exactly true. I think over time your mind, to protect its own sanity, covers the wounds with scar tissue but the emotional damage remains with us, and we never quite forget what we went through. In saying that, over time I was able to rediscover who I was. I managed to get my old self back which was something at the time I thought was beyond possible. And believe it or not I have managed to find an unexpected positive; a silver lining if you like, from all this. I am now equipped with an invisible super-power – I can spot a manipulative, charming, egotistical narcissist a mile off and I won't ever fall foul to one again.

CHAPTER 4

VICTIM MODE

It is common practice for most narcissists to have a victim mode setting programmed into their mentality. This, among various other reasons, makes it very difficult for outsiders to see them as an abuser due to their high levels of self-pity. Essentially, playing the victim role means that the narc appears to be the underdog, the misunderstood one, the bullied one, the one that needs your love and support. However, even though the narc may play this role with credible expertise, the facts of the matter couldn't be further from the truth!

Despite the grandiose appearance, narcs have a very low self-esteem. By playing the victim in a story where they are actually the villain, they will inevitably generate much more positive attention than they will negative. Narcissists thrive on this type of attention as it flatters their ego and temporarily raises their self-esteem. Yet, playing the victim is much more tactical than just getting attention from people. Narcissistic individuals are highly skilled at twisting the truth and deflecting the blame onto others. If the narc can manipulate their audience and gain their sympathy, then it makes it much easier for them to avoid accountability and more importantly makes it harder for the real victim in the story to be seen, let alone heard.

'HANNAH'

TURNING THE TABLES

I had had enough, and he knew it. I had been threatening to leave for months and this time, this time I really did mean it. There was never really any one big issue, one massive row or one specific event....it was just everything rolled into one: the lying, the cheating I suspected him of but that he always denied, the heavy drinking and staying out with mates all night, his selfish attitude and the way he twisted nearly every row to be my fault. It was exhausting and mentally destroying me. I simply couldn't cope being in the relationship anymore.

Our martial home was a large contemporary style house with a sweeping staircase that led from the entrance hall to the four bedrooms upstairs. It was a beautiful oak staircase with exposed wood, and I often worried about the kiddies falling but I suppose a tumble down the stairs with or without carpet had the potential to cause injury.

It was a rainy Sunday afternoon, and another row was in full swing. I had gone upstairs to change Lola's nappy on the changing mat in her bedroom and of course he had followed me. Ranting on about everything he does for me and the kids, yelling that I was causing him stress with all my paranoia and that things were all in my head. I knew it wasn't in my head. I knew he was a bully and a narcissist, and I knew it was time to get out. He followed me across the bedroom as I pulled out a fresh nappy from the drawer. He was intimidatingly close, bending over me as I knelt down and by doing so, making it hard for me to get up without coming into contact with him. He wanted that. He wanted me to get mad and push him out of the way, but I had played his silly games for so long now, I knew what he was doing. He wanted me to get physical so he could call the police and accuse me of assault, he could then act the victim and I

41

would look like the perpetrator. It wasn't going to happen. He wasn't going to bring me down to his level, so I simply crawled on all fours back over to the changing mat where Lola lay, thankfully oblivious to the toxic atmosphere. I continued to change the nappy and re-dress Lola, the whole time Rob stood within inches of me yelling and shouting the usual put downs:

"Where do you think you are going because I'm certainly not moving out?"

"Do you think you'll get another man to take you on?"

"Who would want a fat, crazy bitch like you?"

I'd heard them all before, many times truth be told. Once upon a time they would have hurt me, made me question my own mind and my own sanity at times but now, now they just rolled in one ear and straight out the other. I think that's the thing about being with a narcissist – once you realise what they are, when you truly understand their selfish need for control, you can almost switch off to them. You begin to realise that it's not you that has the problem – it's them and so it tends to become much easier to ignore their words, or at least was did for me.

Lifting Lola back into my arms and managing to avoid any physical contact, I left the bedroom and made my way downstairs. No sooner had my foot touched the bottom step when I heard him yell "I WANT TO DIE" as he flung himself down the staircase! Given that the staircase was a sweeping one he didn't manage to get very far and as I turned around, I was just in time to see him land in a bent heap about 7 steps down! Even though this pathetic attempt at suicide had clearly not worked out for him, the scene itself was still alarming and by now my other daughter Olga aged 6 had appeared from the TV room to see what all the commotion was about. As I tried to gather the kids together and get them away from this distressing sight, Rob started kicking the walls where he now lay clearly in a state of unnecessary aggression. Getting the kids settled I quickly grabbed my phone, now panicked by the sudden shift in the seriousness of the situation, I called our neighbour.

"Betty's coming cover Rob" I shouted up the stairs "You need to calm down! You can't do this in front of the kids!"

I was scared now. I could feel my heart beating in my chest because I knew phoning for help was a big NO NO. I'd wanted to call out to someone many times over the years, but I knew that doing so would have severe consequences. I understand now that a narc never wants to be exposed and so involving other people in our private business was always strictly off bounds and Rob had his ways of always making sure I kept my mouth shut.

Within minutes Betty came running through the front door and into the hall. She had a look of utter confusion on her face as the only words I'd managed to get out during the brief and frantic telephone call was "I need you over here! It's Rob!"

The poor woman hadn't a clue what she had just walked into, and I didn't have any time to explain because as soon as Rob heard her voice, he picked himself up off the stairs where he had landed and ran back into Lola's bedroom. I raced up the stairs with Betty following me and as we rushed into Lola's room the sight was unbelievable. There was Rob curled up in the foetal position in the middle of the floor crying…no not crying…. he was sobbing. Sobbing uncontrollably causing his entire body to shake while he cradled his head in his hands. He looked like a broken man whose world was falling in around him. However, looks can very often be deceiving when you are dealing with a manipulative narcissist!

Betty turned to me with a shocked and concerned looked on her face and asked.

"What's wrong with him?"

I struggled to think of an answer that would explain the torment I had been enduring at his hands for years, but I came to the conclusive answer and said "I've told him that I want a divorce. The relationship is over".

Betty immediately knelt down by Rob's side and began to sympathetically stroke his arm while offering words of comfort and understanding to the apparent inconsolable Rob. I looked on, completely astounded at the twisted version of the truth that was unfolding before my eyes.

Within a few minutes, Betty's husband Bill had arrived, clearly aware of the frantic phone call that had taken place between Betty and me minutes earlier.

"Is everything ok over here?" he asked, clearly puzzled and alarmed by the sight of Rob curled up on the floor like an infant crying as his wife gently offered her empathy and support.

My jaw was on the floor. I couldn't believe what I was witnessing. I honestly stood there utterly speechless as both Billy and Betty aided Rob to his feet and each one taking an arm as if they were cradling a critically injured victim, they lead him down the stairs. As they gently guided Rob out through the front door, Betty turned to me and said "He's having some sort of breakdown. He needs a doctor. Best he come with us, and we'll calm him while we wait for an ambulance. Billy, you ring the ambulance will you dear. There now Rob it's going to be ok……"

What on God's green earth did I just witness? An Academy Award winning performance no less! There I was, stood in my hallway, front door still lying open, watching on as Billy and Betty almost carry an apparent poor, helpless Rob down the front steps and across the garden to take refuge in their house while they wait for medical attention.

WHAT THE HELL! I wanted to shout. THERE'S NOTHING WRONG WITH HIM! HE'S ACTING AND YOU ARE FALLING FOR IT! HE IS NOT THE VICTIM HERE – I AM!

Of course, no such words came out of my mouth as I was rendered speechless.

I know that what I witnessed that day was nothing more than a performance of gross manipulation. Rob had yet again turned the tables to play the victim while I was painted out to be some cruel villain who was causing poor, vulnerable Rob stress and anxiety over my unnecessary and unwarranted demands for a divorce. I dread to think what Betty and Betty must have been thinking!

When a narcissist is backed into a corner and can't escape, they will go to unimaginable lengths to save their own skin and of course their image. I had asked Rob for a divorce, and he didn't like that. His anger and aggression towards me were having no effect at changing my mind. It angered him further that I was not reacting to him or getting into the usual twisted and tiresome arguments where more damage could be done. Rob could sense a shift in dynamics and feared that I might actually be serious this time. Me leaving him and filing for a divorce meant there was a risk he would be exposed for what he really was. A nasty, selfish, angry and aggressive man. A stark contrast to the image he portrayed so well to the outside world. The risk was high and realising that he wasn't going to be able to bully or intimate me into changing my mind, he needed to change tactics and quickly. So, angry, aggressive, abusive Rob suddenly changed into vulnerable, suicidal, VICTIM MODE Rob faster than a greyhound out of a trap.

Amazingly not only did Rob refuse medical attention that day, but he left Billy & Betty's house after a cup of coffee which seemed to, in Betty's own words *'miraculously cure him.'*

Rob claimed that it had just been a petty misunderstanding and that he had been under a lot of stress at work. Promising them he would speak to his GP he thanked them for their help and concern and made his excuses to leave.

Did I go ahead with my plans to file for a divorce? No. Why? Simply because it's just too damn hard. He is a master of manipulation and no matter what I do he will always be there, twisting the truth and shifting the blame. I've learnt to live life separately from him as best I can. I adopt the Sloth Approach and just get on with life as it happens. We don't exchange many words these days and I've taught myself to shut down when he starts on one of his rants. I no longer care when he doesn't come home or the binges that he goes on. Some days I'm ok, other days I'm a broken mess trying my best to make sense of it all. Not the best way to live I know but I'll gather the strength to leave one day. One day I'll get my life back. They often say that a good woman stops loving the man long before they actually leave. If that's the case, then I'm halfway there already.

CHAPTER 5

ZERO TO ONE HUNDRED

It is undoubtedly safe to say that nearly every narcissist is quick to anger. They can literally go from zero to one hundred quicker than a toupee in a hurricane and often in circumstances where such an extreme reaction is disproportionate to the situation.

When you attempt to stand up to a narc or challenge their behaviours or actions in any way, your bold and brave decision to do so is like a red rag to a bull. The instant loss of control the narc feels is often displayed in an outburst of inappropriate rage. They perceive that their very being is under threat and they switch almost as quick as lightening to protect and preserve their image, their ego and of course, their control.

You must always remember that a narcissist has a very low and often fragile sense of self-esteem and despite how they may act in public, they are deeply insecure individuals who possess a constant need for positive reassurance and attention in order to feel good about themselves. A narcissist will never allow themselves to delve into or confront their insecurities. Instead, they convince themselves that they are better than everyone, believing they are more important than those around them and therefore deserve to be treated with admiration and respect. This misconstrued perception of themselves drives their desire and need for constant positive attention and so anything other than your praise and gratitude is seen and felt by the narc as negative.

Negative feelings are a trigger for narcissists as they evoke feelings and emotions of being unwanted, unloved, criticised and unappreciated which are often linked to their past/childhood traumas, and which sadly have never been addressed or dealt with. They don't want those inherent emotions dragged up nor do they want to feel the shame and inadequacy associated with them, so they react in an adverse, horrific and often explosive way to regain their control and authority over the situation.

When a narcissist is challenged by someone, they immediately feel they are under attack and their reaction can be instant anger, lashing out with no consideration for the consequences or the feelings of any individuals who may be in the firing line.

These explosive outbursts may take the form of shouting and screaming, throwing things, making hurtful remarks, threatening to hurt you, others or even themselves and can sometimes turn to physical aggression and abuse.

You must also note that a narcissist has no empathy. They will not foresee or consider how their uncontrolled rage and anger may make their victims feel and sadly far less do they care. They will feel no shame or embarrassment, nor do they have any remorse for their actions.

'LAUREN'

POOLSIDE ATTACK

It was 2014 and we were off on our first foreign family holiday. Our daughter Amy, aged 5 at the time, was so excited as it was going to be her first time on a plane and neither myself nor Patrick had been abroad together before, so I was really looking forward to a week in the sun.

Was my marriage happy? Not really. I always felt something wasn't right but could never quite put my finger on it. The dynamics between myself and Patrick were strange, and I always felt like I was walking on eggshells around him. He had never been physically violent towards me, but he had a temper, one that was attached to an extremely short fuse that could explode for no apparent reason, as I had witnessed first-hand many times.

Anyway, back to the story.

Having arrived at the hotel very late in the evening, all I wanted to do was crawl into bed. Poor Amy had worn herself out with all the excitement over the airport and being on a plane for the first time. She had the window seat which brought her great delight as she excitedly pointed out everything she could recognise from her bird's eye view. Patrick has spent the entire flight asleep with his ear pods in, but I didn't care, I was quite content watching Amy's face light up when she realised we were in the clouds.

She had fallen asleep in the taxi on the way to the hotel and was now slumped over my shoulder, not even aware we had arrived at reception. We got checked in and our bags were taken up to our room by the hotel's porter. I had just tucked Amy into bed when Patrick announced he was going for a dander. It was past midnight at this stage and although I thought it strange that he would want to go for a walk on his own, leaving me and Amy in the room when we had only just arrived, I also knew not to question him. Patrick hated it when he was questioned. He would immediately become very defensive, and that frighteningly quick temper of his would show in his eyes. So, I said nothing and myself and Amy snuggled down for the night.

Of course I couldn't sleep. I was aware of every noise and voice outside our hotel room. I watched as the minutes ticked by on the clock beside my bed which slowly turned into hours. It was past 3am before Patrick returned to the room, a strong stench of alcohol following him. Not even bothering to see if I was still awake, he simply rolled into bed fully dressed and went to sleep. I knew not to say a word. My head was thinking all sorts…. where had he been? Who had he been with? Why would he leave me and Amy like that? This is our first family holiday and he's acting like we aren't even here!

Truth be told I was used to this sort of thing happening back home. Patrick's idea of going out for a few drinks would mostly end up in him drinking so much he wasn't fit to bite his own finger. He often would end up not coming home until the next morning, claiming that he slept on a friend's sofa. Not the way I had pictured married life to be, as I'm sure you can imagine.

I didn't know many of Patrick's friends, not really. I knew them to see but Patrick had never been the type to introduce me formally or socialise with them and me together. I was always kept separate. That's just the way it had been from the very start of the relationship, and I suppose I just accepted it. So now, here I was lying in a hotel room in a foreign country with the same thing happening. I kick myself now for putting up with it. But then hindsight is a wonderful thing.

The next morning after breakfast we got settled by the pool managing to get a couple of loungers close to the edge so that I could keep a watchful eye on Amy. She had taken a few swimming lessons in preparation for the holiday but wasn't overly confident, so I made myself comfortable on my lounger knowing she was in my line of vision while Patrick simply popped in his earbuds which were attached to his phone and took out a newspaper. I remember thinking how can he listen to music and read the paper at the same time?

Wouldn't he much rather play with Amy in the pool and enjoy being together as a family instead of acting as if we weren't even here. But again, I said nothing.

After about an hour in the pool Amy decided she wanted to get out and as she approached our sun loungers to get her towel, she leaned across Patrick's newspaper managing to drip a few drops of pool water onto the open pages. His annoyance and rage were so immediate that they even took me by surprise. He lashed out and grabbed Amy by her arm, violently shaking her.

"You bloody clown! Look what you've done!" he spat out through gritted teeth, almost inaudible so the fellow sun bathers either side of us would not be alarmed by the obvious venom in his words.

Amy stiffened in fear, recognising Patrick's angry glare her eyes locked onto mine. It was a look I'd seen her give me so many times and a look that a child should never have to display – especially when the cause of it is her other parent. It was a look of complete and utter panic! Not fully understanding what crime she had committed, she stood, frozen in silence as her eyes started to well up. Patrick, upon noticing that a few people close by had slid their sunglasses further down their noses and were looking in our direction, obviously curious as to what or who was causing the commotion, released his grip on Amy's arm. Amy quickly wrapped her towel around herself and sat down quietly at the other side of my lounger placing herself as far away from Patrick as possible.

My reaction was one of shock and confusion. Why such a severe reaction to something as harmless as a few water drops on a newspaper which was going to be discarded after he'd read it anyway. I was also shocked that he had carried out this display of uncontrollable rage in such a public area; usually it's only me and Amy that see that side of him behind closed doors. He was always very charming when we were out in public but maybe it was because we were in a foreign country. Half the people watching probably couldn't even speak English and perhaps, in the knowledge that he was never going to see any of them again, his guard was down.

The moment Amy sat down I turned to Patrick and said calmly,

"Your parents must have been very hard on you if that's how you treat a child".

Those words – that short little sentence is one that I will never forget saying. Even thinking about it now I can imagine myself right back there all those years ago. The warm sun, beautiful surroundings, the other holiday makers and my poor, scared and embarrassed daughter sitting beside me.

No sooner had the words left my mouth when Patrick reached for the drink on the table between our two sun loungers. Before I had time to comprehend what was about to happen, he launched the entire contents of the drink in my face! Right there in front of everyone not to mention our 5-year-old daughter!

"DON'T TALK ABOUT MY PARENTS" he spat in my face. He was so close I could smell the remnants of booze off his breath from the night before. He grabbed the newspaper and after folding it in half, he tucked it under his arm and made his way through the throng of sun loungers to the poolside bar and found himself a seat. Once comfortable he unfolded his newspaper, ordered a drink from the waiter and proceeded to carry on with his reading as if nothing had happened.

WOW! I was speechless, utterly humiliated and profoundly embarrassed. I could feel eyes on me, eyes of pity from the other holiday makers who were positioned directly behind me. They had no doubt felt the spits of overspray because whatever didn't manage to hit me directly in the face was sent in droplets in their direction. I smiled an apologetic smile at them. No one wanted to approach me. No one wanted to get involved in the obvious domestic.

I could feel the tears of humiliation starting to sting the backs of my eyeballs. I remember looking over at my bewildered daughter and again saw that familiar look of fear in her eyes.

My heart broke for her, for myself and my unborn baby. Yes, I was 6 months pregnant when this happened. He did this to his pregnant wife in front of his 5-year-old daughter.

Now, it will only be the readers who have experienced narcissistic abuse who will understand that this apparent major incident was simply brushed under the carpet and the day continued as if it had never happened. Amy and I were somewhat subdued and back to walking on eggshells for the remainder of the holiday, but nevertheless it was simply accepted, and we moved on.

If you have experienced a narcissist, you will know the Jekyll and Hyde personality they possess. Their ability to act in such a cruel and harmful manner, rage rushing through their veins like venom and then in literal seconds change into a completely different person. A calm and reasonable persona suddenly appears, and they begin using their gas lighting tactics to convince you that it was somehow your fault.

Apparently, I had pushed his buttons that day by mentioning his dead parents. I had embarrassed him in front of all those people because I was so loud and aggressive with him. I didn't feel I had been loud or aggressive, but he was too busy talking *at* me that I didn't get a chance to defend myself.

He said he was annoyed with me for siding with Amy and not backing him up when he attempted to deliver any sort of discipline. He started bringing up previous rows and said that I do it all the time and it makes him feel inadequate as a parent. I wanted to tell him that the discipline he delivered

61

far outweighed the crime, but I didn't speak. I just sat there and listened. I started to feel guilty and began to question myself at this point. *"Did I really do that?" "How long had he been feeling this way?" "Oh gosh I really should learn to keep my mouth shut!" "It was all my fault!"*

Throughout that 6 night holiday, Patrick got hopelessly drunk on 5 of them, disappeared on two evenings only returning to the hotel room in the early hours of the morning, lost his temper with Amy countless times over petty things, insulted me about my makeup, promised he would stop drinking when we got home, told me he loved me more than life itself and that he couldn't possibly live without me. Oh, and then he blatantly flirted with one of the air hostesses on the plane home. His behaviours were giving me such radically contrasting messages it left me feeling like I was losing my own mind.

I was mentally exhausted. I didn't know if I was up or down, staying or leaving, crazy or sane, but like I've said before, those of you who have experienced this form of psychological abuse will no doubt be reading this story and nodding your heads in agreement, saying to yourself:

"Yip. I've been there."

I know many of you, especially those who have not encountered a narcissist, will think that I should have left then and there, took Amy and got on the first plane home, packed my stuff and marched myself straight to the divorce courts. But you see I had been subjected to this sort of thing, this abuse for so long, so subtly over time that I was so lost. I had no certainty in my own mind because I had become accustomed to feeling both confused and devastated by his behaviour on a regular basis. My self-love and self-esteem were so low that I didn't see the toxic environment I was living in as his fault any more than I saw it as mine.

We travelled home and you might be surprised to read that life continued in the same way as it had done for some two or three years more before I was finally able to escape. The aggression, the disrespect, the selfishness, the constant insults followed by extreme bouts of affection and attention which would then flip back into silent treatment and ignorance of my very existence continued. My marriage was

63

nothing more than a trauma bond. This man that I had married with the genuine intention of being with for the rest of my life had somehow created a world of confusion, fear, loneliness and daily anxiety that left me unable to recognise the woman I had become. I was lost.

When the marriage did finally end, I spent several years trying to figure it all out, going over events and situations in my mind – much to my own detriment. Countless hours of sleep have been lost and I have the wrinkles and under eye bags to prove it! Thankfully I've stopped all that now as I finally recognise that I was never the problem. It was always him. So, I have left Patrick firmly in the past and in doing so I got to meet me again. I'm glad to report that I'm very happy in the company I'm in.

CHAPTER 6

SHIFTING THE BLAME

If you ever find yourself in a situation where you are confronting a narcissist about something they have said or done, just watch how quickly they turn it around and make it all about you!

Taking accountability for their actions is not something a narcissist is capable of doing. They will stubbornly refuse to take any responsibility and instead will attempt to wriggle their way out of accepting blame by any means possible. Even when you present them with evidence of their wrongdoing, or if you try to explain the undeniable facts of what you saw or heard, they will still refuse to accept any accountability.

When you challenge a narc's behaviour, the narc perceives that challenge as a personal attack on the over-rated superiority they feel about themselves. They thrive on feeling powerful and in control so when someone is attempting to take away that control and make them accountable for something they have done, the narc will react in a negative way.

If you are ever in a situation where you have witnessed unfair, unkind or aggressive narcissistic abuse, directed either at yourself or someone else, my advice is to not get into a discussion about it. You are certainly correct and within your rights to challenge them on their wrongdoing and make it clear that you don't consider their behaviour or behaviours as acceptable, but this should be delivered by way of a simply statement and then where ever possible, remove yourself from the situation.

Saying things such as:

"I don't appreciate your tone and so I would prefer if you didn't talk to me about this anymore"

"I don't like how you are behaving, so I am no longer prepared to engage with you right now"

"Your perspective is interesting; however, I know what I saw"

"I know what I heard, and I am not prepared to have my mind changed by you"

It is more about you acknowledging their narcissistic behaviours and promptly shutting them down. Ultimately you want the behaviours to stop and cutting them off or refusing to engage with them will help you to achieve that goal. At the same time, it will send a clear message to the narc that you have boundaries which you aren't prepared to break. Remember, narcissistic individuals are masters of manipulation, blame-shifting and gas lighting and they will do whatever is needed to avoid taking responsibility for their behaviours. Don't let them provoke you into reacting and at all costs try to avoid getting into a verbal exchange with the narc. Nothing you say is going to make them take responsibility and all you are doing is creating a situation which will ultimately leave you frustrated and exhausted. The narcissist will not back down and proceeding to argue with them is as pointless and as futile as a chocolate teapot!

'CRAIG'

<u>YOU MADE ME DO IT</u>

I remember that day like it was yesterday, not that I care to remember it at all you understand. Funny that isn't it; how the bad memories seem to have a way of sticking around much longer than the good ones. It is a known fact that our memories and our emotions are inextricably linked in the brain. This means the more unpleasant, disturbing and emotionally traumatic events which we experience tend to stick around in the memory bank for longer than those events that bring us joy and happiness and those which are emotionally uplifting.

Traumatic memories get stuck in a small area deep within the midbrain called the amygdala which is the part of the brain that is associated with your fight or flight mode and feelings of fear and anxiety. It is basically a processing centre for our negative emotions. I learnt this on one of the rare days I actually paid attention in school. However, continuing with my studies in neurological science to become the world's best brain surgeon was never on my agenda. So although I am unable to pass on any more insightful words about the hows and whys of our unfortunate ability to remember with such ease our past traumatic experiences, I will say this; it's a pity the Big Man upstairs didn't foresee how that particular in-brain wiring issue may cause potential problems when he created Adam and Eve. The Bible teaches us that God shares the pain and suffering of everyone; well, he could have made things a lot easier for himself, not to mention all of us living on Earth, if he had corrected that psychological oversight and made us in a way that our memory banks could only hold good memories, and the bad ones were banished for all eternity. Maybe if I ever reach the big pearly white gates myself, I will endeavour to have that conversation with him.

The day in question was two years ago now. Two years and four months ago actually, thanks to my amygdala! Yet despite my life being completely different now, I can still remember the feeling of utter devastation, shock, and anger, not to mention the reprehensible brass neck she had and how she managed to speak with such confidence – like she truly believed her own words!

It was about 6pm on a Thursday and Mel had been in the shower when her work colleague Susan had pulled up into our driveway. I had attempted to let Mel know by shouting up the stairs, but she was unable to hear me between the sound of running water and the music that was blasting through her phone from within the bathroom. She always took that bloody thing with her everywhere. It was as if her life depended on it being by her side 24/7. If you asked me what her screen saver picture was, I wouldn't be able to tell you. My view was always that of the back of her phone as I watched her taking endless selfies or scrolling through her various social media platforms as if missing something would have some sort of catastrophic impact on her life.

Still stood on the doorstep after refusing my offer to step inside, Susan had appeared quite flustered. She explained she was in a terrible hurry and that she had been speaking to Mel earlier to arrange for her to call over and collect some work report or something.

That was just typical of Mel. She was always making some arrangement or other and never letting me know. I mean how hard is it to communicate with your partner? Evidently for Mel – it was very hard. I was never told anything! She never once discussed her work or her friends. The only reason I knew who Susan even was is because she lived in the next street to ours and we would have bumped into each other in the park when we took our dogs for their daily walk.

Mel had always seemed quite…I don't know…secretive I suppose, like she never opened up to me. Anyway, since Mel seemed to be uncontactable as she discoed in the shower, I had offered to get the report for Susan myself and immediately went to look for Mel's work bag. I didn't have to go far before I found it hanging over one of the kitchen bar stools. I could easily see the folder in question wedged into the bag, so I had grabbed it and handed it over to a very grateful Susan.

It was only after Susan had left and I returned to the kitchen that I noticed the small white business card laying on the floor. It must have fallen out of Mel's bag when I grabbed the work file. I picked it up and was immediately alarmed by the fact that it wasn't a business card but an appointment card. An appointment card for a private health clinic in Belfast and the appointment date neatly written on the reverse read Tuesday 2nd @ 4pm.

I distinctly remember trying to gather my thoughts as to why Mel would have a medical appointment at a private clinic and not even mention it. Not talking to me about work and friends was one thing but a potentially serious medical issue was something I should have been told about as her partner.

It's funny how the mind tends to go fuzzy when we learn about something that gives us a feeling of shock and alarm.

It's almost like the brain can't quite regulate our feelings and questions simultaneously. Our thoughts and words start whizzing about in our heads like an episode of Looney Tunes as we try to make sense of it all. I remember a lot of thoughts were being thought; was she ill? Was it serious...... was she *pregnant*? We hadn't been trying or anything, but you know, these things can happen when you least expect them. I needed to find out what sort of clinic this was and fast!

I remember hearing Mel's footsteps coming down the stairs as I had begun to type the name of the private medical clinic into the search bar on my phone, and as if by ironic perfect timing, she appeared right in front of me just as the distressing results popped up.

I looked her straight in the eye and said, "Why did you have an appointment at a private Sexual Health Clinic last Tuesday at 4pm"

I'm actually surprised I managed to verbalise the question out loud considering the state of shock I was rendered in. Of course, I knew exactly why she had made the appointment – people don't go making random appointments at sexual health clinics unless they thought they had caught or had been in a position in which they may have caught, a sexually transmitted infection.

You probably won't believe it but the first thing she said to me was "I didn't". Just straight up denial. Funny thing was the appointment card had her name and date of birth neatly written on it, so I wasn't buying that as her answer. I managed to stay quite calm considering the situation I was in. My hands were shaking, I remember that much, but I didn't raise my voice or get all lairy at her. I did keep looking at her though, to see if I could sense anything from her reaction, but she seemed emotionless which left me feeling more confusion than anger. I was just too God damn gobsmacked to be angry…at that point anyway.

I asked her again, calmly, why she had an appointment for a sexual health clinic, quickly followed by another more relevant question which was: "Have you cheated on me?"

She didn't answer the first question but was quick to reply to the second with a stern No! I didn't believe her. The atmosphere in the kitchen was strange and I had started to feel a very profound sense of unease. Something wasn't right and my gut was telling me that she as lying.

I had taken a seat at the kitchen table by this stage, and I remember sitting there for what felt like hours but in reality, was probably only a few minutes, just repeating the same question to her over and over.

"Have you cheated on me?" "Have you cheated on me?"

For some time, Mel appeared quite unworried…relaxed almost, which again gave me a feeling of great unease given the circumstances we appeared to be in. She just kept saying "No" as a response to my repeated questioning. However the task of repeating herself soon started to take its toll on her volatile temper and as she grew more frustrated with the constant repetition of dialogue, I knew I was getting close to her breaking point.

I had begun to sense a shift in her manner at that stage; she knew she was caught! The evidence was damning, and she knew she was unable to deny it or even come up with a plausible reason for booking the criminalising appointment. It was as obvious as the day is long that she was guilty. She had cheated on me and now she had to take responsibility for her actions.

"It was your fault! You made me do it!" she suddenly spat out at me.

Clearly her temper had reached its boiling point and the relaxed, unworried Mel had quickly been replaced with the angry, defensive one. If finding that appointment card in the first place wasn't enough to knock the stuffing out of me, then that unbelievable outburst certainly was!

There she was, my girlfriend of 18 months, someone whom I was potentially going to settle down and start a family with, brazenly confessing to the immoral act of cheating on me but in some twisted attempt to preserve her own image, she was blaming me for it! Now I am not the type of man to mince my words so I'll tell you straight - right at that point I almost expected a team of reindeer wearing hoopla skirts to fly past my window! I was that shocked! It was MY FAULT! How in the name of all that is divine could her cheating on me be MY FAULT?" I was speechless. Utterly bloody speechless!

She rambled on at me for the next half an hour, unashamedly attempting to explain how the responsibility for her cheating and betrayal lay entirely with me. She started raising issues she apparently had with me which had never been mentioned before, but were now somehow being used as fickle reasons for her deceitful cheating ; I hadn't been paying her enough attention, that I was always tired after work, that I didn't kiss her good morning two weeks ago and countless other pathetic and totally inaccurate reasons as to why the blame for her infidelity should lay at my door. It went on and on as she appeared relentless in her campaign of shifting every last ounce of the blame onto me; I was not affection enough, I was home late from work one night, I made her feel fat, **my name was Craig**!!!

Whatever silly reason she could conjure up in her selfish little mind as she attempted to deflect all the blame of her infidelity onto me, came out of her mouth that evening. Of course, not one answer was given to my questions; who the man was, when had it happened, where did it happen and the most important question of all – what were the results of the SDI tests?

I felt like I was in a whirlwind as she just kept talking *at* me, offering her bullshit lies and stories as excuses for what she had done. After another hour of this crap my head was spinning. I was struggling to keep up with her senseless allegations against me and the confidence in which she spoke was unbelievable. I was switching from defending myself to asking her questions which she cleverly avoided answering by simply throwing another allegation back at me. It was exhausting. I felt confused, then hurt, then angry, then back to being confused again. Eventually I realised that one of us needed to stop this intolerable exchange of words, and acknowledging Mel's incessant attitude of not backing down, it had to be me. I lifted my car keys from the kitchen counter and without saying a word I simply walked out of the house.

In that moment it was very clear to me that I wasn't going to get any sort of honest truth from her and in that moment, I also realised that our relationship was over.

I'm not going to deny it, at the time I was utterly heartbroken. I had thought our 18-month relationship had been a good one. Well, apart from her secrecy, her constant need for attention, oh and that time she flirted with my best mate at a wedding. That particular event was made all the more embarrassing and upsetting for those concerned due to the fact that my best mate had been the bloody groom!!! That had been a messy night! I suppose, truth be told, I had blissfully ignored her flawed and somewhat worrying characteristic traits in a bid to keep the relationship. Sad, I know. However, even with the best will in the world reality soon prevails. My subconscious mind, which I realise now, I had been fighting throughout the relationship, had decided this was the final straw and raising its ugly head to stare me straight in the face, screamed at me to get out of this fucked up relationship as fast as I could.

In hindsight she did me a favour…a massive favour actually.

Although that day had been incredible hard for me and had left me feeling very hurt, betrayed and if I'm honest a little embarrassed, it was also a day of awakening. You see, after the night at my best mate's wedding a few months previous, when Mel had practically thrown herself at the groom, my friends had warned me to watch myself with her. Of course, I had foolishly brushed their words of caution off, not realising at the time that they could see something in Mel that I was blind to. I was head over heels with her and so I had naively put her outrageous flirting down to having had too much alcohol and didn't think anything more would ever come of it. Foolish I know. I should have run for the hills at the sight of that first red flag and not waited for another one.

Fast forward to the day in question when I *fortunately* found that appointment card on the kitchen floor and seeing her standing there in front of me with her bare-faced cheek as she attempted to twist her selfish act of cheating into something I was responsible for, was the slap in the face and the wakeup call I needed. I saw her then in all her glory.... I saw what she really was.... a selfish, narcissistic woman who saw no wrongdoing in her actions and showed no empathy towards me for the heartbreak she had caused.

She never did take responsibility for cheating. In fact, just to twist the knife a little more, after the split she made sure to continue with her web of shift-blaming lies and tell anyone who would listen about how *I* cheated on *her*. Unbelievable beyond belief. I'm just glad I had the sense to end the relationship that day and not enter any sort of peace-making negotiations with her in an attempt to "save the relationship'.

Quite often, one of the hardest parts of being in a troubled relationship, especially when you haven't quite realised you are dealing with a narcissist, is deciding whether to walk away or keep trying. Take it from me, when someone like that waves a massive, big red flag in front of your face – it's never going to turn green! Walk away and don't ever look back.

CHAPTER 7

COVERT SURVEILLANCE

Narcissistic individuals often develop an unhealthy obsession of their ex-partner, with many becoming fixated by them. This is not because they love or value their ex, but simply because, as far as they are concerned, the ex-partner is their possession. You must always remember that a narc considers their source of supply as their belonging; a piece of property to which they hold full ownership. Therefore, they fully believe that it is only *them* who can discard this property; – the property cannot and will not remove themselves from the narc's power.

So, when the partner of a narcissist attempts to end their toxic relationship, as far as the narc is concerned, they are attempting to remove their supply, *their property,* without consent. As I have already mentioned in previous chapters, when a narc finds themself in a situation where he or she starts to feel like they are losing control, they will go to many lengths in order to regain it. We must remember that these types of individuals cannot live without a constant source of praise, admiration and attention and they have an unjustified need to control and manipulate others in order to obtain it.

So, until they have successfully secured a new form of supply, and even in many cases after they have done so, the narc will continue to obsess over their ex, still believing them to be someone they have the right to control.

In many cases, a narcissistic individual will be intensely persistent in their mission to remain in contact with their ex. By using many of their toxic and self-serving behavioural traits such as gas-lighting, manipulation and coercive control, the narc appears determined to succeed in their objective of staying friends, or at the very least of staying in communication. Without this, they are unable to continue their cruel and callous psychological abuse which serves them so well, not to mention the fact that it looks much better to the outside world if they remain on speaking terms with their ex (or ex's). Despite the relationship coming to an end, in their arrogant, self-obsessed and entitled minds the narc will still believe that they can maintain their ruthless control and bullish authority.

As the ex-partner and victim of a narc's abusive behaviours, it is paramount that you disengage and sever all ties with them in order to begin your recovery and furthermore your healing journey. Understandably, you therefore reject their adamant approaches to obtain their selfish alliance and make your position very clear; that you do not want any contact with them.

When you continue to show strength and resilience to their apparent charm or manipulation by blocking their phone number, their social media profiles, etc. and by refusing to have any sort of contact or communication with them, the narc gets weaker. They seek endless validation and attention to compensate for their low self-esteem so, when you withdraw your attention from them and begin asserting your own control, they feel threatened, weak, rejected and vulnerable. These negative feelings are not welcomed by the narc, and they often react with rage and aggression.

Narcissistic individuals are typically chronically stubborn, so when they are unable to achieve their wants and desires one way, their obstinate determination finds them another way. If they cannot obtain a direct supply from you through friendship or regular communication, then they will endeavour to secure an indirect one.

To do this, they may use third parties such as mutual friends, work colleagues and even your own children to glean information; asking about your whereabouts, any planned outings or holidays you may have, or perhaps a potential new partner you might be dating. Any small piece of information they can obtain about you gives them a feeling of power and control. They are primed and ready to twist and turn this newfound information against you or taunt you with it by spreading rumours and lies. Fabricating stories that are very loosely based on fact makes them appear more believable to their acquired audience. Creating situations which are aimed at hurting you, causing you stress and creating an environment where you become weak and vulnerable are also common tactics used by the narc as they attempt to obtain indirect supply. Making false and malicious reports to the Police or Social Services for example or flaunting their new partner in front of you as they maliciously attempt to provoke you. Getting a reaction is their goal; your reaction is attention and that to a narc is their supply.

'JANET'

PICTURES IN THE POST

My relationship with Steve had been a difficult one to say the least. It took me years to finally recognise the psychological abuse and control I was living under and another two years fighting to get a divorce. The way he had been able to abuse the legal system was nothing short of appalling.

My solicitor had asked for his Full Discovery in March when it had been arranged to serve him with my Divorce Papers.

Of course, Steve had ignored that initial request just as he did each and every one that was sent thereafter. I became increasingly frustrated at the rising costs due to the countless unnecessary reminders being sent from my solicitor to his. Even when my solicitor began to word his requests a little more strongly and threaten to take the matter to court, Steve still managed to manipulate things. He was aware that the courts would be closing in June for their summer break and wouldn't re-open again until September, so he delayed and delayed right through from March up until June. Courts closed; nothing we could do.

The Courts re-opened in September, and as you can imagine they were extremely busy. The Judges and Barristers might have stopped working for eight weeks but the world didn't stop turning and the narcs within in didn't stop being massive pricks!

Finally, in late November I got a call from my solicitor informing me that a bundle of Discovery had been received from Steve's solicitor and although he was sure it wasn't everything we had requested, it was a start. A start we had been frustratingly waiting to receive for eight months at that stage.

Later that afternoon, after dropping the kids off with my mum, I made my way over to my solicitor's office. He showed me into a small room across the corridor from his much larger, brighter one and after setting the bundle of paperwork onto the table in front of me, he left me to it. I had requested that I go through the paperwork myself. No offence to any solicitors who may be reading this, but to you we are just another client wanting a straightforward divorce, but to us, the victims of narcissistic abuse, we know that there is never anything straightforward when you are dealing with a narcissist.

I had been visiting my cousin Joe a lot since my separation from Steve and had learnt so much from him. He unfortunately had been married to a narc as well and he had shared many insightful stories of how she managed to manipulate the legal system with her victim persona, crocodile tears and countless delay tactics; managing to turn fiction into fact with her dangerously believable stories and lies. I was only too aware that I needed to give this bundle of paperwork my full attention. I knew Steve and I knew I was dealing with a professional manipulator.

My solicitor had been right, the Discovery bundle received from Steve was lacking to say the least. There was nothing included regarding his business, nor his pension or credit union accounts – not to mention the bank accounts he held in the South of Ireland. Then again, I wasn't expecting to ever get those. Steve was savvy enough to know that the North of Ireland and the South of Ireland didn't share that type of information. Even though we had requested the last twelve months bank statements from *all* the accounts held in his name both North and South of the boarder, we were informed via his solicitor that Steve had no dealings in the South of Ireland and therefore no bank accounts were held. Yeah right.

What we did receive however were the statements for the bank accounts Steve held in the North of Ireland. Well, after all he had to hand over some sort of bank statements so he probably reluctantly chose those ones, although given what I discovered from them it would make me wonder what on earth was lurking within the Southern bank statements!

I made myself comfortable on the small office chair behind the desk and started the meticulous task of going through the transactions. He was good to himself that's for sure; expensive clothes shops, restaurants, hotel stays and the number of cashback withdrawals from Pubs would make your eyes water. That part wasn't surprising if I'm honest, Steve always liked to impress people by buying rounds of expensive whiskeys or shots. He thought people went out socialising with him because they liked him, but it was probably more to do with the fact that a night out with Steve was the equivalent to a free bar!

About four pages into the bank statements, I noticed a transaction for a rather large sum and printed beside it appeared to be the business name it was payable to. It was a name I didn't recognise so I put a red pen mark beside it thinking I would query it with the solicitor later. However, when I continued onto page five I noticed another transaction, again for a very large amount and with the same business name beside it. Seeing two of these substantial amounts going out to the same unknown company made me start to wonder so I quickly took my phone out and googled the name of the business. I'm glad I was sitting down at the time because my knees immediately turned to jelly, and my hand started to shake. I can remember thinking 'No. No, he wouldn't. He didn't. No'

What was staring back at me from my mobile phone screen was a website for Private Investigator Services.

Despite the now uncontrollable shake in my hands, I quickly scrambled through the remaining pages of Steve's bank statements only to find to my utter horror seven more transactions to the same business. I was totally shocked, frightened, horrified not to mention upset. This discovery unnerved me to the point of tears, and I remember thinking instantly of my kids, feeling aa sudden overwhelming protectiveness towards them. It was one thing paying a private investigator to follow me, but what about the kids? They were often with me so had they been followed as well? So many thoughts, questions and emotions surged through my mind in those next few moments.

I somehow managed to stumble to my feet and without even pausing to knock, I walked straight across the corridor into my solicitor's office. He looked up from his desk as I approached, clearly startled by my unannounced entrance. I remember him looking at me with concern as I can only imagine my face was whiter than snow as I mumbled something, which was probably barely audible, about what I had just discovered.

I cannot begin to tell you the chronic paranoia that took over me from that day. Almost instantly I became a bag of nerves jumping at the slightest movement and noticing every single sound around me. I felt like I was unable to focus on anything but yet my senses had me convinced everyone else was focused on me. It was extremely unnerving and frightening.

My solicitor was shocked at my alarming discovery of the Private Investigator. He told me he had only ever dealt with one other case involving a PI in his 30 years as a Solicitor and that was from a man who suspected his wife had been cheating. This husband had employed a PI to follow his then wife to obtain the evidence which he would need to successfully divorce her on the grounds of Adultery. It had worked. The evidence obtained by the PI was used in Court and the husband was granted his divorce from his cheating wife. In some way I could understand the reasons why that husband had employed one of these Private Investigators to follow his wife. He clearly had a strong suspicion of her infidelity and knew he needed convincing evidence to prove it. However, I couldn't understand what Steve's reason was. We had been separated for nearly two years at this point and he even had himself a new partner. Yet from the payments recorded on his bank statements, this PI had been following me within the last ten months which didn't make any sense to me or my solicitor.

It was agreed that we would send a letter immediately to Steve's solicitor requesting a full explanation regarding the reasons behind these payments made to the Private Investigator and copies of any such reports or evidence that was obtained by them.

Surprisingly, we didn't have to wait long this time for a response. The full PI's report arrived in the post to my solicitor's office the very next day. It was almost as if Steve was proud of the fact he had been covertly watching me and was keen to show off what he had gathered. No reminder letters were needed this time as my solicitor received the full PI report including many images along with a covering letter from Steve's solicitor which stated:

We are aware from your client's bank statements that she has been in receipt of Single Parent Benefits since her separation from our client. Our client informs us that he believes your client is co-habiting with her new partner whilst in receipt of these benefits. Our client therefore employed the services of a Private Investigator to obtain evidence of such which he has forwarded to the HMRC.

WTF! This was crazy! This was just complete made-up bullshit. Steve wanted to destroy me. He wanted to cause me as much stress and harm as he possibly could and I'm not going to lie – he managed to do just that with maximum effect.

The Private Investigator's report which had been forwarded to us gave detailed descriptions of not only my comings and goings, but also those of anyone else who had visited my home while they had me under surveillance. It showed pictures of me going back and forth from my home at various times of the day, the PI having clearly followed me on several occasions and had included photos of me or my car as evidence. Details such as times and vehicle registrations were included as the report gave information on my various locations such as the local post office and on one Friday evening when I went to the chippy for a take-away. I could not for the life of me understand the logic in this trivial and frivolous information. As the weeks continued it was evident that they had become even more intrusive. Photos had been taken using a high zoom lens through the windows of my house as they attempted to identify any prospective co-habiting partner. One photo in particular was of my then fifteen-year-old daughter in her bedroom after her return from school. The contents of this PI report were nothing short of sickening. I was overwhelmed with feelings of rage and disgust. I found it immensely difficult to comprehend how anyone, anyone at all, let alone the man I had married, and the father of my children could instruct such an act. How could he request such a cruel and unnecessary invasion into not only mine, but to my children's, my friend's and my family's privacy for the pathetic and irrational reason of reporting me for potential benefit fraud – of which I was completely innocent. I was physically sick that day – right there in the bin at the back of my solicitor's office. I have never in my life felt so incredibly vulnerable and angry at the same time.

Despite my emotional state I had so many questions whizzing around in my head.

Who took these photos?

Are these Private Investigators vetted or regulated in any way?

Could they have more photos that they have kept for their own sick perversions?

Did they see me or my kids undress?

Do they show these photos to others?

But most of all the question that kept returning in my mind was 'How could he?'

Despite having the awareness that Steve was a narcissist I still couldn't quite believe that he would stoop to this level.

For the days and weeks after I had viewed the PI's report, as you can probably imagine, I didn't sleep. I went from being a happy woman, finally free from her narcissistic husband to a paranoid wreck. I became totally convinced people were following me. I would stare at every car that drove past my home looking to see if they were holding up a camera. I became wary of every stranger that glanced my direction in the shops and instead of trading my usual pleasant smile, I would glare at them with suspicion.

I was aware of every noise and creek around the house to the point that I found it impossible to sleep. If I did manage to nod off it was short lived as the intensely realistic and frightening dreams that seemed to have taken up permanent residence in my head would swiftly wake me. My curtains were permanently pulled tight and socialising with friends stopped almost immediately. My mental health deteriorated at an alarming speed which in turn caused considerable stress and worry to my kids and immediate family. Thankfully my mum encouraged me to go to the GP who prescribed me some anti-anxiety medication as well as sleeping tablets and advised me to seek some trauma counselling.

It was awful. I was living a nightmare all because some selfish, nasty, inconsiderate bastard thought that he might be able to land me in a bit of trouble with HMRC. That never did happen. I'm sure whoever was unlucky enough to open Steve's letter at the Benefits Office, containing the PI report attempting to report me for co-habiting, thought it must have been some sort of joke. The photos and daily reports of my comings and goings gathered by the PI proved nothing. Yet somehow, in Steve's delusional mind his thought process must have been very different. What *was* his thinking? Did he think that if he managed to cause me an intolerable amount of stress and worry that I might become vulnerable and weak, giving him the opportunity to be the one to swoop in and save me? Did he think that if he got me into trouble with HMRC for some sort of wrongdoing that it might make him look better in front of the Judge and possibly win the divorce?

I'll tell you what he didn't think; he didn't think about the kids. He didn't think about the knock-on effect of having our house put under surveillance would have on them. The stress they would endure watching their mother grow more and more unsettled and anxious with every passing day. He didn't think about the sleepless nights, the paranoia and the immense worry he created. He didn't think about anyone but himself.

To this day I will never know why Steve made the decision he did to hire a Private Investigator and put me and my family through the cruel and unnecessary invasion of our privacy that he did. Of course, I reported the whole sordid affair to the Police, but they couldn't help. Apparently Private Investigators are *'a grey area'* within the Law and unless they have entered my property or approached me pretending to be someone they weren't, then there wasn't anything the Police could do to help me as no Laws had been broken.

These Private Investigators are legitimate and registered businesses. However, the Police did inform me that pretty much anyone can set up a PI service – no vetting or Police checks are needed. So basically, it would seem that even a sex offender could be a Private Investigator if they so wished and offer their services to the unknowing public! I would be pretty damn sure that anyone who is vindictive enough to employ one of these PI's isn't too bothered about checking their CV's! Utterly mind-blowing when you think about it.

It still shocks me to this day that me and my family were put under surveillance like that and despite Steve's story that it was done so he could accuse me of some wrong-doing, I am inclined to think it was just to exert his dominance, control and authority and of course to keep a close eye on me because I truly believe in his twisted, warped mind he felt it was his right. Whatever his reasons, all I know is that you can never, ever underestimate a narcissist. They will adamantly attempt to destroy you and ruthlessly dismantle your mental health to selfishly feed their over inflated sense of superiority, their need for power and their undeniably selfish desire for control.

* * * * *

CHAPTER 8

COLLATERAL DAMAGE

One of the saddest things about a narcissist is their lack of empathy for others. They don't think about anyone else but themselves and this sadly doesn't change when it comes to their children. Narcissistic individuals are unable to possess the natural paternal bond that genuine, empathetic people do. They don't feel a connection to their offspring and will instead see them only as an extension of themselves – something they own, control and have rights over. A narcissist will see their children as their property rather than individual human beings with a mind of their own.

Sadly, children are often the default victims of a narcissistic relationship and can suffer from low self-esteem, emotional imbalance, self-blame, anxiety and abandonment issues. As they reach adulthood, they tend to struggle with identifying their self-worth and many find it difficult to establish healthy relationships for themselves. During their childhood they have been exposed to the narcissistic traits of their parent and for this reason they often don't understand that they have a right to set boundaries any more than they can identify the red flags associated with a toxic, narcissistic individual.

Never stay in a toxic relationship for the sake of the children. LEAVE for the sake for the children.

ISLA'S STORY
<u>UNFORGIVEABLE</u>

Dave came into my life when I was just a few weeks old. I hadn't known my biological father as he bailed the minute he found out my mum was pregnant. Apparently, he wasn't ready to be a daddy and rather than stick around and be a crap one, he left, which I suppose when you look at it wasn't the worst thing he could have done.

My mum met Dave through mutual friends and so when things moved pretty quickly in the relationship, she sort of felt it was ok. Although she hadn't known him long, she had known *of him* for a few years through the mutual friends and so this contented her. If he had been an unsavoury sort, then surely her friends would have warned her. Lesson one here; don't judge someone by other people's standards – often they don't really know them, especially if the person in question is a covert narcissist.

They moved in together after a few months and things progressed from there quite quickly onto a spontaneous engagement and a whirlwind wedding. Not long after the *'I Do's'* had been said and mum's surname was changed to Smith, it was decided that my surname should also be changed to align us all as a family, and from that day on Dave became my Dad. Obviously, I don't recall any of this legal paperwork being carried out, all I knew is that I grew up as Isla Smith - daughter to Dave and Margaret Smith.

Obviously, as a child I couldn't comprehend that Dave was a narcissist, all I knew is that our home was regularly a battlefield. Slamming doors, spine chilling yells from Dave compounded by the puffy eyes of my mum were a regular addition to my childhood. One of my earliest memories is when I was in primary school, and I remember how Dave would insist that the top button on my school shirt was fastened, checking it himself every morning before school, telling me that I would not embarrass him by going into school looking like a scruff. That top button almost choked me, but Dave didn't care. He had a look – a very intimidating look that made sure you did what he said.

He was like an Army General, insisting that every part of my uniform was perfect, and insisting that my shoelaces were untied before I took my shoes off was one of his strict rules. I sadly learnt the repercussions of breaking that particular rule when Dave appeared in the doorway of my bedroom one evening holding my school shoes in one hand and a pair of kitchen scissors in the other. I had made the mistake of slipping my shoes off that afternoon rather than untying the laces. Dave didn't say much that evening, but then he didn't need to as he proceeded to cut the laces into tiny pieces as I stood there looking on at the deliberate destruction of my innocent school shoes with astute shock.

He did smack me, I know that. During those primary school years, I used to suffer from what the doctor described as 'night terrors' where I would appear to be awake, screaming or shouting but I was actually still in a deep sleep. I think I used to frighten my poor mum half to death when she would hear my alarming yells from the bedroom and rush in to find me sitting up in bed, eyes wide open but totally in the land of nod. She would be unable to comfort me, and the doctor had advised to just make sure she created a relaxed bedtime routine and to offer me reassurance when I woke. Looking back on things now, and the toxic environment I was growing up in– it's no wonder I was screaming in my sleep!

Dave did not like his sleep to be interrupted, and knowing this my mum would often dash out of bed as quick as her feet would carry her into my room as she attempted to calm and quieten me before waking him up. There were occasions however, where Dave managed to beat mum to it. He would storm into the room, nostrils flared with temper and annoyance at being woken up by my harrowing cries. I would always remember the next part as I was brutally awakened from my night terror by the sharp slaps Dave would be delivering on my bare legs.

"I'll give you something to scream about!" he would shout at me.

I won't ever forget the sting of those slaps.

When I was about seven or eight years old, we were preparing for my First Holy Communion. Dave was always front and centre at these types of events. Always full of smiles and loving the attention he got from neighbours and friends telling them how pretty I looked in my dress. It was funny though, because when it was just us, Dave wasn't so smiley. I just always remember him as cross. After the service in the local chapel had ended, and the school photographer had taken a few pictures, we headed into town to a fancy restaurant for a meal. For dessert I had ordered a bowl of mint choc-chip ice cream which of course being an eight-year-old child, I accidentally dropped a bit of green coloured ice cream across the front of my communion dress. Dave was so cross. He got super mad at me and said I had spoiled the dress and that I was a silly, foolish, lazy little girl who didn't deserve ice cream and so he slid the bowl angrily away from me and proceeded to finish every last bit himself. The tears stung the back of my eyes, but I knew not to let them fall.

After the meal, mum had suggested that before we go back home, we call with my Aunt Dee who was unable to make the communion service, to show her my beautiful dress - now sporting a small green stain created by the dot of mint choc-chip ice cream on the front. During the visit, Dave took a phone call and as soon as he ended the conversation with whoever was on the other end of the phone, he announced that we had to leave. I remember he was very abrupt about it, causing my aunt to look at him with alarm.

"Is everything alright?" she had enquired, but her concern was quickly brushed aside by Dave who assured her everything was ok as he gathered the coats and headed for the front door, me and mum in quick pursuit behind him.

Once outside and safely in the car away from the concerned look and earshot of Aunt Dee, Dave announced that it had been the vet on the phone.

My heart sank. Our dog Sheba, who mum had had long before I was even born had been quite poorly lately and the vet had prescribed some medication and told us not to take her on any long walks and that he was hopeful she should improve.

Mum had been quick to ask Dave the question that was already on my mind,

"Why was the vet calling you?"

When Dave replied, I immediately burst into floods of tears, as did mum. Dave had phoned the vet and asked him to call out to the house to euthanize Sheba. I was heartbroken, confused and so desperate to get home and see Sheba I remember leaning forward in my seat and grabbing mum by the arm, begging her to make this stop.

"No! No mum! Please don't let him do it! Please!"

The rest of the car journey was a blur of tears and raised voices as mum tried to plead with Dave not to do it but Dave argued back that the dog was old and the medication was too expensive to keep continuing with. Words, tears, shouting….it was the most horrific car journey I think I've ever had.

By the time we pulled up into our driveway the vet's van was already parked up beside the dog kennel. I leapt out of the car, desperate to stop the vet, to grab hold of Sheba and keep her safe, protect her from what was about to happen.

"Go upstairs and take your good dress off Isla" Dave commanded.

"But…. but…I want to see Sheba" I stuttered out through my tears.

"Do as I say and then you can come down and see her"

His word was final. There was no point in looking at mum for backup because I knew only too well that she was no match for him. I ran up to my room as quick as I could, fighting with the buttons on my dress with every step, flinging it over my head and grabbing the first piece of clothing that came to hand, pulling it on and racing down the stairs and back outside.

I was too late. It had been done. Sheba was dead.

I won't every forget that day and the misery and anger I felt. Dave didn't care while me and mum were utterly heartbroken.

Now, as hard as that day was, I'd love to be able to tell you that it was a one-off occurrence and I don't have any more cruel, upsetting and horrible stories to tell you about how I suffered at the hands of Dave, but unfortunately, I can't. You might also wonder why I have referred to my 'Dad' as Dave throughout this story and what I'm about to tell you might just answer that question.

My mum stayed with Dave for another four years, but when I was twelve, she suddenly decided enough was enough and she moved out and filed for a divorce. Of course, this decision was not taken well by Dave, and he began an escapade of torturous phone calls, threatening text messages and controlling behaviours such as refusing to pay any child support. Being a self-employed individual, this was something Dave could very easily do, and subjecting my mum to more anxiety was something he seemed to take great pleasure in. Not content with creating financial distress for us, the ranting, angry phone calls still continued. It was on one of these abusive, raging phone calls that Dad became Dave.

My mum had shown immense strength and resilience to Dave's bombardment of abuse and manipulation, and this was angering him even more. He wanted control and he couldn't get it, so his interest turned to me. He wanted me. I mean, he didn't really want me, he just wanted to take me off mum because he knew that would cause her pain and suffering. He had never so much as done a homework with me or taken me to the swimming pool in my twelve years of existence, so why on earth did he have a sudden interest in me now: to exert power and control as every narcissist does.

Mum wasn't giving in to his demands to have me and her phone was lighting up constantly as he relentlessly rang and rang. Eventually mum answered the phone and as we were driving his voice came through the Bluetooth speakers loud and aggressive.

Immediately he started shouted,

"GIVE ISLA TO ME! TURN YOUR CAR AROUND RIGHT THIS MINUTE AND BRING MY DAUGHTER BACK HERE"

Mum obviously had no intention of doing any such thing, but the more she refused to obey him the angrier Dave became. His voice had become barely audible at this stage – it was just angry noise.

Then suddenly, there was a calming silence. Dave had stopped shouting and for a moment we were all silent. When he spoke again, Dave's voice was calm and clear.

"I'll tell you what. You keep her. You keep your precious little Isla, what do I care. Isla…" he continued, "…if you're listening to this, which I'm sure you are then know this; I'm not your real dad and I want nothing more to do with you."

Silence.

Deafening silence

The phone line went dead as Dave hung up the phone. Mum immediately slowed down the car and pulled into a side street, turning off the ignition she turned to look me straight in the eye, her face already wet from tears.

"I'm so sorry. I'm so utterly sorry Isla"

I looked at her, tears now free flowing down my cheeks and said,

"It's ok mum. He didn't deserve me anyway."

CHAPTER 9

THE SLOTH APPROACH

There is a term used by psychologists and therapists when offering guidance on how to deal with narcissistic people which is referred to as *The Grey Rock*. It is effectively a method of non-emotional, limited contact which the victim should utilise when communicating with a narcissistic individual.

When I started studying narcissistic abuse and I first came across the term Grey Rock, I'll admit that I wasn't overly keen with the analogy. This was mainly due to the fact that we are humans with emotions, abilities and a sense of self, not some lifeless, hard, cold grey matter. The comparison didn't seem right, so for the purposes of this book I will refer to this non-committal approach as 'The Sloth Approach'......at least we can identify some similarities i.e. a heartbeat at the very least!

So, what is 'The Sloth Approach'?

It is a technique used by those who find themselves dealing with toxic, abusive or manipulative individuals – everything a narc can be. The theory behind the technique is that the victim becomes as unresponsive and unengaging as possible until the abusive or toxic person loses interest.

This may mean avoiding eye contact, giving short, straightforward responses to questions or text messages and most importantly – showing zero emotion.

Think of yourself morphing into a sloth and embracing their chilled out, non-committal personality. Sloths are not creatures who engage in drama or conflict; they don't jump like a deer at the slightest movement in the bushes or fight to the death to prove their hierarchy. Instead, they hang around motionless or move about slowly, appearing to not have a care in the world.

The Sloth Approach is something you should utilise as a communication method when you are either unable to or preparing to move to the No Contact Rule. You need to be unreactive, show no emotion and if a response is absolutely required take your time to think about what you have to say – not what you want to say.

When dealing with a narc The Sloth Approach is not only a necessary and practical way to minimise interaction, but it can also be an aid in helping you to detach yourself from their emotional pulls – often referred to by the professionals as hoovering.

How long you must use this approach won't necessarily be in your control as it will depend on how long it takes for the narc to get the message. They will of course attempt to push beyond this new boundary you have built, but you must resist all temptations to let your emotions rule your mouth or your fingers. With this in mind, you cannot adopt The Sloth Approach on a part-time basis. You cannot appear to be unengaging for two or three weeks and then go on an emotional or angry rant at the narc the following week. This isn't how it works. Just like the No Contact Rule which we will cover in the next chapter, it's all or nothing – no half jobs, no coming and going. You are not a yoyo, and swinging back and forth will only serve as allowing the narc availability to you which means you are opening the door to them and giving them the opportunity to manipulate, love bomb, guilt trip or harass you. When you begin to set boundaries with a narcissistic it is imperative that you maintain them. Bending or breaking them only gives the narc more power and demonstrates a weakness on your part.

Remember what you are dealing with. A narc will never change, so as long as they have a form of communication or contact with you – whether that be face to face, phone calls, text messages or even through a third party, they will continue in their attempts to abuse and manipulate you. Keeping this at the forefront of your mind will help you on the road to complete freedom and recovery.

In summary, The Sloth Approach is a method of minimum communication which you can use when attempting to distance yourself from the narcissist and can be a stepping stone before you move on to the No Contact stage. Going No Contact means you fundamentally disarm the narc of their power and control over you and you can begin to regain your life.

'VICKY'

<u>PHONE FEAR</u>

I'd been doing so well, at cutting the contact I mean. It was hard at the start because I used to get a lot of anxiety when he would send a text message or ring me and I wouldn't respond. That part was harder than I ever imagined it would be. This man had hurt me in so many ways, I despised his very existence, yet I almost felt obligated to answer him. That part was difficult for me to get my head around – the control he still seemed to have over me even though I had made the step to separate from him. But I understand now that it was out of fear rather than obligation. I feared what might happen if I ignored him or if I angered him because I had seen his anger so many times before. He didn't like it when I ignored him, when he didn't get his own way. I knew what he was capable of and how little it took to send him into a rage.

Now, back home living with my parents I felt safer. He couldn't hurt me anymore, not physically anyway but I still had that fear of the consequences of not responding to him. I'm not going to lie, it was incredibly hard and it took time to build up the confidence to ignore him. I guess that's understandable given the years and years I had spent with him treating me as he did and always getting what he wanted one way or another.

We were going through Family Court to sort out an access agreement for our three children. I had tried to sort this out without the expense of court bills and solicitor costs, but it was impossible. He would change plans at the last minute, send me several messages in between contact sessions which were often about the children, but I honestly felt they were unimportant or something he could have easily asked the children themselves.

"Does Noah need to wear his glasses for watching telly or just reading?"

"Those packed lunches you made for the kids this morning look awful! I wouldn't feed that muck to my dog!"

"Do you know if Jessica has swimming on Thursdays?"

"I might be 5 minutes early for the kids today as I'm getting out of work at 4.30 instead of 4.45 due to me having to stay late one night last week for a meeting which overran"

These messages came every week without fail. Some were just pointless questions, others were a dig at my parenting or my cooking and some were telling me things I didn't even need to know. Why do I need to know that he was keep late at work one evening last week? Why would he think I needed to be told that information or that I would even care?

I knew it was just to keep me in his life, but I swear every time my phone pinged with a new message alert, I could feel my heart start beating a little faster, my anxiety heightening.

120

I used to try leaving it for an hour before reading it but that just made it worse…...my anxiety lingered the full hour, a little voice in my head kept saying *"What is it now? Is it good or bad? Will it annoy me, upset me or is it just another pointless message?"*

Of course, he knew what he was doing. He was keeping me as his supply. He hated the fact that I'd left him and taken the kids, he hated the fact that I called him a narcissist yet here he was displaying one of the very traits of narcissism – holding on to his supply for as long as possible.

After about six months, Family Court had pretty much come to an end and agreed contact was put in place via a Contact Order. This gave him specific days and times when he would collect the kids for contact and exactly when he was to drop them back home again. During those six months I had worked hard on reducing my replies and responses to his messages and phone calls. It took months of work on my part. I started off by ignoring messages, then he would ring my phone, so I blocked his number from calls. In the beginning I kept him on WhatsApp because I thought I had to in order to arrange access for the children, but it was just the same old nonsense. Silly messages at all hours of the day and night – thank goodness I didn't have a new partner! What on earth would he think?!

The messages were showing no sign of decreasing even after the court had granted the Access Order but, by this stage, I was now stronger and my self-esteem was finally getting a step back up from the gutter where he'd managed to put it over the years. Finally, the day came when I was brave enough to block him on WhatsApp as well. He now had no direct contact with me whatsoever.

I'm not sure what he thought about this sudden show of strength and independence on my part. He was now unable to send me his usual messages to rant or scream about it but I'm 100% certain he didn't like it! Id taken control of the situation and typical of a narc, he hated not having control.

As predicted, he then started to send messages via the kids.

Tell your mum this and *ask your mum that* when the kids returned from a contact session. This still annoyed me, but I found it much easier to handle and didn't suffer the same anxiety I did when my phone was pinging a hundred times a day! I had achieved what I once thought was impossible. I had cut all contact with the narc meaning his supply was no longer available upon his request and there was very little he could do about it. The narc had been defeated and I was elated!

Then the *Parenting App* was introduced.

During the Family Court proceedings, the Judge had instructed that the court appoint a Court Liaison Officer, who was basically a qualified Social Worker to speak to the children on a number of different occasions. Myself and my ex were both given her work mobile number for emergencies just in case we needed to change any dates or times of any of her visits with the children etc.,

Now, again typical behaviour of the narc, my ex took it upon himself to contact the Court Liaison Officer reporting that he was having a few difficulties communicating with me.

He told her that I had become hostile and had blocked him on all forms of communication. He felt this was 'detrimental' to the ongoing contact approved by the Judge. Oh boy, he knew exactly what to say and how to charm the birds from the trees. Unfortunately, this Court Liaison Officer clearly had never dealt with a narc before, and her inexperience shone through as she fell for it - hook line and sinker!

So here she was on the other end of my emails, having copied in my ex, both of our Solicitors and the Judge, suggesting that in order for the access to continue smoothly both parties – that's myself and the narc – should download the *Parenting App* and recommended this be used to utilise contact between both parties.

All my hard work, all those months of building up the courage and strength to remove him from my life only for a professional to literally put him right back in my face again…not just my face but into my head!

No sooner had I read her email when my phone pinged with a message from her. She had forwarded me a text from my ex with the link to join him on the *Parenting App*. He must have had it already downloaded and here he was – keen as mustard to get me to join him on this supposedly great communication app.

A quick phone call to my solicitor and my worst fear was confirmed.

"It's better to follow all directives from the court otherwise you could be seen as being hostile and causing deliberate tensions which may be deemed by the judge as unnecessary." He informed me.

So, there you have it – the professionals were once more dancing to the tune of the narc, and I was the unheard victim once again.

That bloody Parenting App was the very bane of my existence. I think it was on my phone for all of about 6 weeks before I completely lost it one day and hit that delete button with gusto. He had used it to degrade me, to control me, to dictate what I should do with the children when they were with me, to make endless suggestions about meeting up or having a day as a family 'for the sake of the children'. It was relentless and my mental health was right back where it was when I was with him. My anxiety was through the roof, and I started to hate taking my phone with me anywhere I went but the practicalities of work and being contactable for the kids outweighed my desire to throw the bloody thing into the first lake I found!

I did consider contacting the Court Liaison Officer or my Solicitor to discuss my concerns, but I had since lost all faith in their understanding of my situation, least of all their ability to see that my ex was a narc!

So no, I just did it myself, and I'm pleased to say I took immense pleasure in hitting the delete app button whilst he was in mid flow of typing one of his weekly rants!

No court in the country can make a grown woman have contact with another adult and I only wish I had recognised this sooner and been strong enough to say NO to that Court Liaison Officer! If the Judge saw my decision of cutting direct communication with my ex as being hostile, then he would need to invite me back into court where at least I would have a chance to explain myself and show the rants, endless messages and coercive control being displayed by my oh so charming ex!

So, the lesson here folks – when you are dealing with a narc don't expect everyone else to see them as you do, not even the professionals. Don't be afraid to stand up for yourself and what you know to be the truth despite how much they may try to just make you 'get on with it' or be civil 'for the sake of the kids'

No one will ever quite know the narc the way you do so never let them make decisions for you.

Not wanting to leave my story on a sad note, I'm pleased to say all that was two years ago now and I have remained NO CONTACT since. My life is immensely better for it.

CHAPTER 10

NO CONTACT RULE

I want to begin this chapter by being unreservedly frank with you. The most important lesson we, as empathetic genuine people need to learn is that you can NEVER stay in contact with a narcissistic individual post separation. I should point out that this is also true if the narc is a family member, friend or even a work colleague. The NO CONTACT RULE applies to all narcissists.

It is common for narcissists to seek out vulnerable individuals who are easily fooled by their apparent endearing charm. Many of these individuals are quick to form emotional bonds as the narc begins their tactical 'Love Bombing' phase, lavishing attention and affection on them appearing to be the Mr or Mrs Right they have been looking for. Once the narcissist has used their fake self to attract and sadly trap an empathetic individual, that person becomes the narc's supply. The narc has gained the trust and devotion of this individual and in doing so has secured what they now see as an unlimited source of attention to feed their emotional needs and exaggerated sense of self-importance. Before long the impending insidious abuse begins. The Narc will ultimately strive to be in a position of power, so they begin to use various techniques such as gas lighting, coercion, blame-shifting and humiliation to undermine and weaken this new found source of supply. The weaker the individual becomes the more powerful the narc feels. So, as the victim begins to lose their self-esteem, their independence and confidence, the narc begins to feel they are in a more favourable, powerful position. Having control over their victim feeds their ego and they selfishly indulge in the situation they have created.

When someone has become a form of supply to a narc and ultimately their victim, the narc sees them as someone they can control, dominate, exploit and use for their own selfish fulfilment and it's important that you understand this. So despite the breakdown of a relationship, the narc will endeavour to keep their victim on a backburner, forever in the mind-set that they were and always will be a source of supply to them.

They will use every opportunity to continue with their pattern of manipulation and control regardless of the fact that the relationship has ended, and this can even be the case when they have secured a new supply from someone else. Supply is supply to a narc and they will never stop seeking it from whichever sources are available. So even when you end a toxic and abusive relationship with a narc, they may still unashamedly attempt to remain in contact with you.

If you have been a victim of narcissistic abuse you would no doubt be happier than a pig in shite to see the back of the person who has undoubtedly broken your heart, messed up your mind, attempted and very probably succeeded in financially burdening you, caused you mental and sometimes physical scars and ultimately left you a shell of the person you once were before you met them. However, due to the delusional mind-set of a narcissist, they don't ever see things from anyone else's perspective but their own. They will go to great lengths to ensure you both remain friends or at the very least stay in some form of contact with each other. This is not because they have changed or matured, it's not because they suddenly value you as a person – it is simply to maintain their supply.

Another reason why the narcissist may want to stay in contact is because when a victim attempts to cut all forms of contact and communication it gives them an opportunity to free themselves from the narcs control. With each passing day that they are free from the narc, their own reality starts to emerge. This is a far cry from the distorted and unpleasant one presented by the narcissist. Things start to become much clearer to the victim and it is at this point they often feel immense rage towards their abuser as they start to realise what has been happening to them. This is not something the narcissist is comfortable with as it risks them being exposed for what they really are. If the narc can continue to gaslight and manipulate their victim, the harder it is for the truth to be revealed. Image is extremely important to the narcissist, and they want to maintain their false identity to the outsiders, so being seen as remaining friends with ex partners helps support and feed their fictional persona. They don't *want* you; they *need* you!

The supply that a narc gains from his or her victim is symbolic of their control. Let me explain this a bit more. When a narcissist contacts you after a breakup, and despite the fact that you have zero interest in being friends with them, by responding to their message even under some sort of feeling of obligation you are giving them supply. The content or context of your response is irrelevant. It doesn't matter if your response is negative or positive it's still a response and to the narc it is pleasing. You have given them attention/supply and to them that's all that matters.
You need to understand that whatever the narcissist's message may be; good, bad, remorseful or desperate - it has been orchestrated simply to get a response. It is your response that feeds them. They feel control when they know they have your attention. They know that you have put time and thought into responding, good or bad - it doesn't matter, your attention is on them for that minute, or half an hour or for whatever length of time you are engaging with them. So even when the relationship has ended, and you are no longer living with or associating with them, you are still giving them your attention and providing yet another desperately desired boost to their ego. That's their only goal.
By maintaining communication with a narc post separation, you are ultimately keeping the door open to a highly skilled, unscrupulous professional manipulator who will, without doubt, lead you into another phase of your life that you will

live to regret, and your much desired narc-free life is nowhere to be seen.

A common tactic used by the narcissist throughout the relationship and again after it has ended, is to take on the role of the one who wants to move forwards. They want nothing more than for you to forget about all their past misdemeanours and in doing so may often offer words of encouragement such as:

"It's not good for you to live in the past"
"Don't go over old ground again, I've said I was sorry for that"
"You need to learn to move on and let the past stay in the past"

While this may all sound like good advice, the narc is only offering it on a selfish level. They don't want you to remember or remind them of all the nasty, cruel and hurtful things they did. They know this will only serve in making their mission of staying friends with you much harder to achieve.

So, they attempt to convince you they care about your wellbeing, that they have changed, learnt from their mistakes and will endeavour to make a fresh start and never, ever repeat the same behaviours again. THIS IS ALL LIES. All they are attempting to do is draw you back in.

This *nice* behaviour you are witnessing is nothing more than a combination of Hoovering and Love Bombing. They may even use Gas lighting to convince you that you are remembering events differently or that things you know to be true are false.

If you share children with the narcissist then you can be pretty sure they will be brought into the equation and used against you as you try to oppose any sort of friendship/ contact with the Narc. Attempts will be made to shame you or guilt trip you into forgiving them and being friends 'for the sake of the children'. This is why I often speak on my social media pages about the benefits of using the Family Court system to sort out child contact arrangements. I'm not blind to the fact that courts can be extremely stressful never mind expensive, but when you are dealing with a narcissist it's the only way to enable you to go NO CONTACT. While you remain in direct contact with the narc to organise child access, you are never going to be narc free. Read that again.

The narc might display emotional vulnerability to make you feel pity for them. This is a standard personality trait of a narc who is a master at playing the victim and is carried out in order to manipulate you and, of course, pull on the strings of your empathetic heart. Don't fall for it – it's all an act!

If you cast your mind back to the beginning of your relationship with the narc, you can almost see the same pattern occurring now as they use the same tactics, as they attempt to maintain some level of contact with you after the relationship is over. Remember how they used Love Bombing at the beginning of the relationship to sweep you off your feet with excessive flattery and over the top gestures of love and romance. Remember how they played the victim card on more than one occasion to gain your sympathies and your trust, appearing to open up about their alleged past heartaches. Then, slowly the Gas lighting tactics came into play and before you could click your heels 3 times you were spun into an indescribable, toxic, and often traumatic relationship.

These are the narc's weapons and so it makes perfect sense that they will rely upon this arsenal post-separation just as they did throughout the relationship.

It's important, as genuine empathetic people that we educate ourselves and become wise to these tactics imposed upon us by narcissistic individuals.

Going NO CONTACT means you are taking control of the situation and putting boundaries in place as soon as possible which will inevitably save your energy, your peace of mind and ultimately your mental health.

When you establish NO CONTACT, you need to remove all forms of communication which the narc can potentially use to reach you. Blocking them on social media, phone calls, WhatsApp, etc. will deliver a very clear and strong message to the narc - you are totally, 100% in control.

Despite the clarity that this message serves to deliver, we do have to appreciate that we are dealing with a narcissistic individual who will always want things their way and won't be willing to compromise and accept your terms of No Contact. For this reason, you need to be prepared for the many attempts they will make to break through your boundaries. Using other people such as mutual friends or family members to obtain information about you is common. They might turn up at your place of work or to a social event where they know you are going to be. Whatever tactics they deploy as they attempt to break through your barriers – don't falter! It's vitally important you stay strong and remain non-communicational because letting them in just once will set a precedent that the narc will happily exploit.

For many victims of narcissistic abuse, adopting the No Contact Rule is one of the final steps you can take to regain control of your own life and cut the narc out for good. However, although I've made it sound as easy as a walk in the park, I appreciate that it is not always easy and sadly many victims struggle with initiating a No Contact rule and many more will break it for various reasons. You need to be incredibly strong and focused on what is important – which is YOU!

Hopefully by reading through this book you will begin to see a much clearer picture of the tactical games a narcissist will play which will help you understand that you are nothing more than a pawn in the narc's chess game.

'ROSS'

<u>LOCKED UP</u>

I remember sitting there in horror. A mix of shock and bemusement running through my head, no not just my head – my entire body! What had happened? How did this happen? I'm in a prison cell FFS! How could she do this to me? Why would she do this to me? My job…oh God my job! I'll lose my job! Sam! What about Sam? Would this mean I would lose my son? Why is this happening?

It was September 2020 and Sharon and I had been separated at that stage for six months. Thankfully we never married, but we did have a son together. His name is Sam, and I was utterly besotted with him from the day he was born. Sharon didn't seem as maternal as I once thought she might have been. She liked a drink…or seven and had what I would refer to as a very full social calendar. She refused to breast feed Sam saying that it meant she was restricted when it came to socialising with her friends and I remember at the time thinking that was rather selfish. Of course, I never mentioned my thinking on the topic as I had learnt long ago not to challenge her on anything unless you wanted to be party to a very aggressive outburst.

Sam is just like me in every way, all the same quirky personality traits and funny ways not to mention he has my dark colouring and deep brown eyes. He is obsessed with trains - just like me. Yeah, he is my boy alright through and through and thankfully, so far anyway, at the ripe young age of 9 he doesn't show any of the angry and selfish personality traits of his mother.

Sharon displayed many narcissistic traits throughout our four-year relationship. Unfortunately, I was completely unaware of what a narcissist even was until much later into the relationship and my counsellor mentioned it during a particularly hard session as I tried with immense frustration to describe Sharon's behaviours. I spent the last 8 months of that toxic, soul destroying relationship speaking to a counsellor as I was convinced, or rather should I say, *she* had me convinced that I was losing my bloody mind!

"She sounds very much like someone who displays high levels of narcissistic traits" he had said matter-of-factly.

"She displays what now?" I questioned him with a look on my face that read 'I have no idea what you just said'. I had never even heard the word narcissist before that day.

We spent the rest of that counselling session discussing what narcissism was and how insidiously it played out upon its victims. For the first time everything made sense. Well not exactly sense, I don't think our minds will ever be able to see the sense in a narcissist's behaviour, but things were certainly a lot clearer. The most emotional and transformative part for me was realising that it wasn't my fault. I wasn't to blame. I wasn't going mad. I didn't imagine things, nor had I become paranoid without reason. It was like a light bulb moment from there on in and finally I had clarity – Sharon was a narcissist.

I went home that day with this newfound information but, instead of ending the relationship like any smart thinking person would have, I stayed. 'Why?' you might ask. Well, being in a relationship with a narcissist is like loving your enemy but not quite realising that they actually are your enemy. It's hard to explain but I had this self-destructive trauma bond to her and of course I didn't want to live in a house without my son. It was me who got him up every morning, got him ready for school and made his packed lunch. My brain was so messed up at that stage that I couldn't even contemplate not being able to have my daily routine with Sam. That was probably the biggest reason for staying because of course I knew she wasn't going to make life easy for me when it came to arranging contact if we were to separate.

As it turned out, any decision making I may have had to entertain about ending the relationship, was taken out of my hands. One random Saturday afternoon Sharon announced she was moving out after coldly declaring she had met someone else, taking my boy with her. Just like that my world fell apart. She left that same afternoon leaving me with a broken heart and a colossal fear of what was going to happen next. Just as I had predicted, the first thing she did was to refuse me any access to Sam, so I had to do an application to Family Court. It took every last penny in my bank account that month to pay the court fees and those of my Solicitor and Barrister. They talk about Legal Aid helping but that only seemed to apply for mothers with the children – not the ostracized fathers. I love my son and would have paid any amount to get to see him again, so I lived on beans and tinned custard that month until my next pay arrived.

After a long and arduous court battle with many twisted truths and unfair allegations being thrown from Sharon, I was granted a Final Court Order which gave me access to Sam every other weekend. I was to pick him up after school on a Friday and drop him back to Sharon on the Sunday evening as well as an overnight every Thursday and Friday on the week I didn't see him at the weekend.

I was glad to see the end of Court as the whole process had resulted in me having to borrow money from a few mates just to cover the costs, but it was worth it to be able to have regular, stable contact with Sam. However, I made one huge fundamental mistake which I regret with every fibre in my body. I stayed in contact with Sharon. I thought I was doing the right thing. I thought it would help to accommodate any changes to arrangements, things like dentist visits, school meetings, and birthday parties. All the various things that day-to-day life throws at us. How naive was I?

Sharon became my puppeteer, and I was nothing but a lifeless fool at the end of her strings again dancing to her unfavourable tune. Some messages came in the evening, some in the morning, some on days I was working and some on days I was off somewhere enjoying my time with Sam. She would often ring and shout abuse down the phone criticizing me as a parent because I had sent Sam home with dirty shoes after an afternoon of playing football with his mates in the back garden. Many messages were pointless, and many were provoking – aimed at getting me cross or defensive but all messages were controlling. If I didn't do as she said, like collecting Sam early or agree to changing days at the last minute even though I had other plans, she would simply stop contact and refuse to answer my calls.

Now I thought a court order was final and both parties were to obey the instructions of the court. Not Sharon. Not a narcissist. Three times I was back in court over the space of

5 months – each time because Sharon refused to hand Sam over for some fabricated or petty reason.

The first time she refused me contact was because she said she could smell alcohol off me and Sam would not be safe in my care, even though she had just watched me pull up outside her house in my work van – clearly just finishing for the day. Of course it was total rubbish. I hadn't been drinking in weeks, but it was a game, a tactic to provoke a reaction. When I started to get cross, she said she was ringing the police and that's exactly what she did. She must have had them on speed dial because literally within minutes a cop car pulled up. Trying my hardest to stay calm but clearly agitated by the unfolding events, I tried to explain to a very unsympathetic officer that I had a court order stating I had contact with Sam that day. Meanwhile Sharon, the Academy award winning actress that she is had conveniently turned on the waterworks and was being empathically comforted by the second police officer.

I couldn't believe what was going on and I certainly couldn't believe the police officers were falling for this nonsense. I offered to prove my innocence by doing a breathalyser test which they were more than happy to carry out. However, even when that showed up negative and it was clear I had been telling the truth, the officer said that on this occasion he was going to ask me to leave the property without Sam and make contact with my solicitor going forward.

"Furthermore' he added 'I am giving you a verbal warning to stay away from Miss Bradley until such times as a resolution regarding this matter could be found."

I held my temper as best I could that day, but this was just typical of her. She was highly skilled at being able to put on a show and play the victim so much so that she was able to convince the professionals, in this case the police that she was the victim. The situation was crazy, and I couldn't see how it was ever going to change. I took the officer's advice and went straight to my Solicitor the next morning who informed me that I would have to apply to the court again to have the matter resolved by the Judge. This meant more expense, more time delays and again gave her back all the control. Whichever way I turned she had me backed into a corner, dancing to her narcissistic tune!

The application process to court took 4 weeks. Another 4 weeks without seeing Sam. She knew exactly what she was doing, and it was aimed to hurt me, to break me.

The second time she stopped access, again for some petty reason or other I had to go through the same time consuming and expensive ritual of applying to the court to reinstate the contact order again. I was growing more and more frustrated as it seemed the court wasn't doing anything to prevent her playing these games.

The third time was different thankfully, although it was disheartening to know that she had already caused so much unnecessary suffering and added expense by getting away with it on the first two occasions. When she stopped me seeing Sam on the third occasion, this time was because she had heard through the grapevine that I was dating someone and she felt, "it was not the right time to introduce new people to Sam". The Judge was not impressed. I was still reeling from the fact that she seemed to have forgotten how she left me for another man and that said man was placed in Sam's life the very next day! The hypocrisy was unreal but nothing I hadn't come to expect from her.

That third time in court the Judge did lay down the law to her, pardon the pun. He told her that if she refused to cooperate and obey the court order regarding my access to Sam then she would be held in contempt of court and be punished accordingly. That seemed to do the trick…. or so I thought. From that day on she never once tried to refuse or block my access to Sam. However, unbeknown to me she had something much worse up her sleeve.

I had been on a couple of dates with a girl, early days still getting to know each other, and this particular Saturday night we had gone for a meal in a lovely restaurant in Limavady when, to my dismay, who should walk in but Sharon. Apparently on her own, which made me think she hadn't turned up just by chance, she had followed me. She disappeared among the diners and although it put me on edge knowing she was in the very near vicinity, I tried not to let it ruin my night, so Diane and I continued with our meal. As we finished off our desserts and the last drop of wine in the bottle we had been sharing, a waiter approached our table with the bill. As I prepared to settle up, Diane took herself to the ladies. Unfortunately, she wasn't alone in there. Let's just say when she returned Diane was wearing a raging expression on her face and, waltzing straight over to me, slapped me right across the face in front of everyone before marching herself out of the restaurant. As I regained my balance and the blurred vision in my left eye caused by the slap started to settle, I was angrily aware of a very smug looking Sharon stood right in front of me. The saying Proud as Punch isn't enough to describe the look of pure satisfaction on her face in that moment. She was gloating. Whatever she had said to Diane in the ladies had made her slap me so hard I thought my head was going to dislodge itself from my shoulders and be sent sailing across the diner's heads! I saw red. I couldn't help it. This woman, this narcissistic witch had done nothing but cause me misery from the day I'd met her, and I had reached breaking point. I reached out and grabbed her by the arm, pulling her towards me I shouted angrily in her face,

"Why can't you just LEAVE ME ALONE?"

I left the restaurant straight after, totally embarrassed at the drama that had just unfolded. There was no sign of Diane outside, so I assumed she had jumped into one of the town taxis. I drove home feeling a heavy mix of despair, confusion, embarrassment and total hopelessness. I was an emotionally wreck. I couldn't get my head around what Sharon could have possibly said to Diane to make her react that way and for what purpose? Was I not allowed to move on with my life? She had…in fact she had moved on with someone new before our relationship had even ended. I rang Diane several times but to no avail. Every call went straight to her answerphone leaving me with the anguish of my unanswered questions.

I got home and poured myself a very large whiskey. I was a mess. It felt like everywhere I turned Sharon was there, waiting to ruin whatever little thing might bring me some form of happiness. The relationship between us was over yet she still had so much presence in my life, always there when I didn't want her to be, always calling or texting. It felt as if I was her property and as my owner, she had the right to do whatever she wanted, and my rights were non-existent.
I was only home about 45 mins when there was a knock on the door. Foolishly I thought that it was maybe Diane come to make peace as I had been unable to reach her on the mobile. I opened the door, not in fact to find a slightly less

angry Diane than I had last seen, but two unhappy looking police officers.

"Mr Willis?" one of them asked

"Yes." I replied with confusion

"I'm arresting you on suspicion of Common Assault under the Offences against the Person Act 1861, the Criminal Justice Act 1988 and the Crime and Disorder Act 1998. You do not have to say anything, but it may harm your defence if you do not mention something which you later rely on in court. Anything you do say may be given in evidence. Do you understand?"

"WHAT? No, I don't understand! What am I meant to have done?"

It was a long drive to the police station, but after my shameful walk being escorted by two police officers from my front door in full view of all the neighbours, I was more than glad to be out of view of onlookers.

I was processed, fingerprints taken – the whole nine yards as they say. Just like it's done on the telly. I was placed in a cell to await the arrival of my solicitor.

Those 56 minutes seemed to last forever. Sitting in that cell I contemplated my life, and it wasn't pretty. I can honestly say that if it wasn't for having Sam, I would have been quite happy to leave this earth that night. I was done.

I was charged with Common Assault on Sharon as a result of me grabbing her arm in the restaurant. The evidence she provided of the bruising on her arm was most certainly something she had inflicted upon herself because I knew I had not applied enough pressure to cause those marks. Nevertheless, she was believed as per usual and there was nothing for me to do but accept defeat.

My Solicitor had initially advised me to plead Not Guilty but when counsel for the prosecution informed us that Sharon had requested that she give her evidence via video link due to the *'emotional distress and the fears for her safety'* that she felt, I changed my plea. I thought to myself I'm not playing her game for a second longer! No chance! I did grab her arm that day – I accept that I'm guilty of that – however it was maliciously and deliberately provoked and the alleged injuries sustained were in no way reflective of the pressure applied. Given the fact that she had clearly charmed the professionals again and wanted to continue with the elaborate drama by giving her evidence via video link, I decided it best to not dance to her tune anymore. I wasn't going to give her her day in court which she clearly wanted to use as a playing field to further humiliate and criminalise me. I pleaded guilty meaning I was able to remove her stage.

I accepted the charges and swore to myself that from that day forward I would have zero contact with her.

From that day on I made a promise to myself. Never again under any circumstances would I even as much as look in Sharon's direction. She was a wicked, dangerous and callus individual who was prepared to stop at nothing to destroy me. She had no empathy for what she had done and didn't care about the damage or hurt she had caused. I blocked her number on all forms of contact as well as blocking her profiles, so she couldn't see or communicate with me through my social media accounts. I also arranged for a solicitor's letter to be sent to her stating that going forward any communication that she may need to have with me had to be delivered via her solicitor. That took the wind out of her sails. She wouldn't be so quick to ask her solicitor to send me the nasty and manipulative message she was prone to sending me.

Two weeks into the No Contact rule and there was an immediate shift in my mood. My anxiety and stress levels decreased almost overnight proving to me that I should have gone No Contact a very long time ago.

I can only imagine the frustration Sharon must have been feeling not being able to get in touch with me as easily as she had been able to before. Her calls were blocked, her messages were left undelivered and following a reset of my privacy settings on social media, she couldn't even stalk me from behind a screen anymore. I'm sure the blood vessels in her neck must have been pulsating round the clock!!

But, as always, a narcissist wants to win and Sharon, clearly desperate to get my attention had one last party trick up her sleeve. Fourteen days had passed since that day in court when I pleaded guilty to common assault and fourteen glorious days of No Contact. On the days when Sharon was due to drop Sam off at my house, I had not gone to the end of the drive to greet him like I used to. This had always given her an opportunity to start a row or make vile comments towards me so, as part of my No Contact rule I had decided that I was no longer prepared to walk to the end of the driveway as this removed the opportunity for her to start anything. Instead, I opened the front door and waved at Sam to come on in. The first time this happened I could see the bewildered look on Sharon's face as she sat in the driver's seat, clearly confused at my seemingly unbreakable determination to stay away from her in all circumstances. She wasn't used to this. The tables were being turned and it was now me making the rules. No communication, no stalking and now no physical face to face encounters at drop off. I can only imagine how infuriating this was for her but I didn't care, I was protecting myself and it was working.

It was the regular Thursday afternoon drop off and the sun had made a rare appearance. I heard Sharon's car pull up outside my house bang on 3 o'clock. As usual I simply opened the front door and stood in the doorway waving to

Sam to come in. Sharon, who seemed to be getting used to this new ritual simply turned around in the driver's seat to say goodbye to Sam as he jumped out from the backseat. As he made his way up the drive towards me, I could see that he was carrying what looked like a casserole dish. I was even more surprised when he reached the front doorstep and raising his arms offered it up to me saying, "Look Dad. Mum made you your favourite chicken curry! Mum says you love her home-made chicken curry."

Well, just when I thought there was nothing more she could possible do that would shock me. What on earth was wrong with this woman?

Speechless. Utterly speechless. Just 14 days ago this same woman was requesting, no not requesting – *demanding* to give her evidence in court via video link against me due to fears for her safety and the emotional stress it would put on her to have to face me. Now, here she was at the end of my driveway waving her goodbyes with a nonchalant smile on her face as our son unwittingly handed me her culinary offering. Unbelievable. Totally unbelievable. That's how they operate, that's how they work when they don't have an audience to appeal to. She wanted to convince the court that I was a man to be feared, dangerous and calculating when in actual fact those were, no not were - *are* the exact personality characteristic of herself and she will never ever change.

In case you are wondering, I didn't eat the curry.... goodness only knows what it might have been laced with!! It was scraped into the food bin and the casserole dish, well it was washed and donated to my local charity shop who were extremely grateful for it.

It sent a very strong message to Sharon too. She has yet to offer me any further culinary dishes after losing one of her casserole dishes. She's obviously had second thoughts about playing that game again! I'm pleased to report that my No Contact boundaries are still firmly in place and every day, every week, every month that passes I'm making steps to getting my life back.

Lesson to be learnt here is that you can never stay friends with a narcissist, despite their many tactical moves to convince you otherwise. NO CONTACT is the only way to deal with them, shut them off, ignore them and never, ever let them provoke you into an uncharacteristic reaction which in my case landed me locked up!

CHAPTER 11

THE NEW SUPPLY

When a relationship with a narcissist finally comes to its bitter end, it can often be surprising how quickly the narc's new partner appears on the scene. Despite the fact that they may still be embroiled in the heinous post separation abuse they inflict upon their ex-partner, a new partner is proudly displayed. It can often be hard to comprehend how they have the mind-set to be able to conduct a new relationship while still holding so much anger and seeming to seek an unwarranted degree of revenge towards their ex-partner but remember – when dealing with a narcissist **anything** is possible!

This new partner is crucial to the narc for two reasons.

Firstly, the narc is always on the outlook for supply – thriving off attention and admiration and, even though they may still be mercifully trying to obtain a supply from their victim after separation, this new partner is being aligned to provide them with a new source of supply going forward. The narc is aware that as their victim begins to cut contact and communication, moving to the Sloth Approach and then onto the No contact Rule, their narcissistic powers become weaker and their ability to maintain a supply from their ex-partner gets smaller and smaller. In this situation, the narc is aware they are in dangerous territory of losing their current supply altogether, and so their need to secure a new one is of paramount importance. By providing the narc with a new supply, the new partner will inadvertently begin to play a crucial role in the narc's self-serving life. They are not important or valued by the narc for genuine reasons such as love or friendship, but simply for immensely selfish reasons; feeding their limitless need for attention, their sense of entitlement, their need for power and control not to mention their over-inflated ego.

The second reason a new supply is crucial to the narc is because, following a bitter breakup, a new partner can unwittingly improve the narc's public perception against any preconceived opinions or judgement from others. The new partner will be groomed by the narc for the sole purpose of enhancing their image – something the narc is prepared to go to great lengths to protect. They will embark on a mission of intense Love Bombing which will be displayed as publicly as possible to capture the attention of others; romantic walks together in their local area, over the top proclamations of love for each other on their social media platforms, expensive gifts or luxury holidays are just a few of the techniques used to obtain the attention of their much-needed audience. This wholly devised display driven by the narc has even more impact when the new supply is the one to be seen sharing it with the world.

The risk of being exposed by their ex-partner after separation is high and so appearing to be in a loving and respectful relationship with a new partner helps to dampen down any potential claims made by the ex that they are in fact a narcissist. Appearing to their social audience as being a calm, rational and happy individual in a new loving and secure relationship is precisely the image a narc will be compelled to portray following a breakup purely for the purpose of protecting their public persona. Should the ex-partner start to speak out about the narc's abusive behaviour and intolerable conduct during and after the relationship, then the blissfully happy new partner acts as the perfect image enhancer for the narc. To further maintain this delusional, manufactured persona, both the narc and the new partner are quick to banish any detrimental rumours which may tarnish his or her image by telling people,

"She just can't get over me"

"He can't cope with the fact that I have moved on, and he hasn't, but I truly wish him all the best"

"Sure, she's not right in the head!"

"He's just bitter that I ended the relationship so he's making up all these lies about me."

"She's so jealous of my new girlfriend. It was her jealously that ruined our relationship in the first place"

It serves the narcissist very well to appear to the outside world as being blissfully happy with a newfound love on his or her arm while making these deflective remarks about their ex. While the victim on the other hand appears upset, confused and angry following the breakup due to the significant trauma they have endured at the hands of the narc. With the help of his or her new partner, the narc is proficient in their mission to convince the outside world that they are the victim and not the actual perpetrator. In summary it is very often the case that the new *supply* is needed and not necessarily wanted.

'GARY'

<u>TWO AGAINST ONE</u>

I thought ending my toxic four-year relationship with Becky was hard, but what came after was much harder.

We had never managed to make it down the aisle, thank goodness, and the house we lived in was rented so that side of the breakup was relatively straightforward to sort out. We simply both moved out of the house and found alternative accommodation – separately. That was of course after a long and lengthy battle with her over who should get to keep our pet dog Ralph.

I loved that bloody dog something rotten. He was a mix between a cocker spaniel and a poodle, with long droopy ears and eyes that would melt the coldest of hearts. I remember the day we got him from the local rescue centre, all scruffy and depressed looking, but I saw a look in his eyes that resonated with me. He had a look that said he needed something better than what he was currently experiencing. It was his sad, yet ever hopeful look that made me think we could both help each other through the tough times, of which there had been plenty throughout the relationship with Becky. Becky had much preferred the prettier dogs in the shelter but as most of those were either already reserved or came with medical issues that Becky was not prepared to deal with, we left that day with Ralph.

The connection between Ralph and me was instant and as Becky drove home not showing much interest in him, I was lavished with doggie kisses and thigh-thumping tail wags. He was overjoyed to be out of that dark, dingy kennel and into the arms of a cuddle-giving, lap-offering human. He needed love and I had plenty to give. However, as affectionate as Ralph was, he never really seemed to warm to Becky though…. I should have seen that as a warning sign!

It's actually fair to say that Becky never did develop a bond with Ralph and never seemed to be particularly fond of him. She hated it when he leapt off the sofa to great me at the door displaying his excitement through his happy bark and frantic zoomies. When Becky came home Ralph would barely lift his head to even look in her direction. Sensing that he liked me much more seemed to spark Becky's obvious jealousy and she would often push him off the sofa when he curled in beside me, clearly unable to cope with the fact that I was getting attention, and she wasn't.

When it came to the breakup, poor Ralph became nothing but a pawn to Becky, a possession she could use with great delight to taunt me with. She knew how much I loved that dog and so she took great delight in taking him from me.

When a narcissist knows you want something, they will do everything they can to make sure you don't get it. Weeks were spent fighting over who Ralph should live with. To me it was a no-brainer; Ralph would come with me, I was the one who fed him, walked him, booked in him for his monthly wash and blow dry at the local dog groomers. Becky didn't even like the dog, but that becomes totally irrelevant when you are dealing with a narcissist. All logic, common sense and fairness go out the frigging window like a wicked witch on her broom on Halloween night! Becky claimed that since her name was on the adoption papers from the rescue centre and on Ralph's vet card then, according to her, the dog was legally hers.

The only reason it had been Becky's name on the documents and not mine, was simply because she was the one with a free hand to sign the paperwork due to the fact that I had always been the one holding Ralph. When I tried to contest her logic, she proudly produced a short letter from her solicitor verifying that he would be more than happy to represent her in a custody battle should the need for one arise. It was pointless, but still, I spent a lot of time and energy debating with her, even begging her at one stage to let him come with me until I realised it was just another game to her. Another excuse to exert her control over me one last time. She seemed to revel in the knowledge that what had begun as negotiations between us over Ralph's living arrangements, slowly turned into desperate pleas as I began begging her to just let Ralph come with me, but it was no good. She displayed such arrogance, stubbornness and utter spite to the point I caught myself wondering how I ever thought I was in love with her in the first place.

So, I did what most people do when they are faced with a nasty, bullying narcissist who always had to win, and I let her have him. I let her take Ralph, the dog I knew she never really wanted because I couldn't win against her, and I was exhausted from trying. I just wanted all her deliberate taunting to stop before my head exploded and if that meant losing Ralph then that was just something I was going to have to accept.

I initially moved back home with my parents for a few months as I had some outstanding debts after the breakup thanks to me foolishly allowing Becky to use my credit card for her many luxurious and often excessive spending sprees.

I stayed with mum and dad until I managed to clear the debts and had enough money saved to put down a deposit on a new rental property. I managed to get a lovely semi-detached house not far from the local park with a small back garden. I remember the day I went to view it, standing in the fully enclosed back garden thinking how Ralph would have loved to play ball here and how much I would have enjoyed his company on long walks around the park.

I had managed to keep my distance from Becky and our paths hadn't crossed since that emotional day when I had packed the last of my belongings into my car and said a tearful goodbye to Ralph. Becky casually sat on the sofa filing her perfectly manicured nails, Ralph whimpered at my feet as I set my key to our rented property on the coffee table beside her. It had truly broken my heart more leaving Ralph than it ever did leaving Becky.

Thankfully, like I say, our paths hadn't crossed since. However, I was always hearing the gossip from mutual friends. Becky had always been partial to playing the victim and so I wasn't in the least surprised when I began hearing various stories of how I had broken her heart when I had decided to call things a day and how she begged me to let her keep Ralph as a reminder of our love. Yawn. Yawn. Yawn. I was bored to tears listening to these second-hand stories. They all varied to some degree but each one focused on Becky's woe-is-me version of events which couldn't have been further from the truth. Thankfully I never allowed these make-believe stories to annoy or upset me. I had learnt a long time ago that getting emotional or angry was just providing her with more attention. So, I never made any comments when these stories were being relayed to me; I just gave a little laugh, a subtle shake of the head and got on with whatever I was doing. If telling these fabricated stories made Becky feel better about herself, then I knew her well enough now to know that no one was going to change her mind. I just kept my head down and got on with life in my new home.

Then one day, in what appeared to be complete and utter randomness, within weeks of moving into this new property who should walk past my front window but Becky with Ralph plodding along beside her on his lead. I was totally overcome with emotion at seeing Ralph and without even taking a minute to think about what I was about to do, I was running out the front door towards the garden gate calling out his name like I was in a scene from Little House on The Prairie. Becky, stopping in her stride smiled at me, appearing to be not at all shocked at my sudden appearance. Funny that! She loosened Ralph's lead to allow him to approach me and even attempted to make small talk with me while a highly excited and very jumpy Ralph licked my face as I knelt down to offer him cuddles. After a few minutes, and upon realising I was now standing in very close contact with my narcissistic ex, I suddenly retrieved my senses and saying my goodbyes to my beloved Ralph, made my way back into my house leaving Becky and him to continue on their way.

About 30 minutes later, as I sat mulling over a now cold cup of coffee, thinking to myself how odd it was that Becky should be walking near my house considering she had set up residence with her new fella across town, when there was a loud knock on my front door. Wondering who it could be, I got up from the kitchen table and opened the door only to be faced with a very heavily built male whom I didn't recognise and a tear-stained faced Becky beside him.

"You giving my girlfriend grief mate?" He yelled at me.

"What? What are you talking about?" I answered, totally confused as to what was going on or who he even was.

"You were giving Becky grief over the bloody dog again, weren't ya!" he spat angrily.

"No, no I wasn't giving anyone any grief....."

I didn't even manage to finish my sentence before this clearly aggressive and angry man, who I could now only assume was Becky's new boyfriend, lunged himself at me pushing his face into mine so closely that I could almost count his eyelashes. He yelled and swore at me, made numerous threats about what he was going to do to me if I ever came near Becky or Ralph again before turning, taking Becky by the hand and marched back out through the front gate, slamming it so hard I was surprised it stayed on its hinges and didn't end up in next door's garden!

I closed my front door and took refuge in the kitchen. I was understandably shaken by what had just happened. I had never even seen this man before in my life. I couldn't understand why he was accusing me of giving Becky grief about the dog. What the hell was all that about? Becky had been fine with me, she had smiled and seemed happy to make small talk but what was the tear-stained face about? I sat down at my kitchen table and poured myself a shot of whiskey. Not what I usually drink at 4pm on a Saturday afternoon but I needed something to calm my nerves and stop the visible shake in my hands, something that coffee just wasn't going to ease.

In the days and weeks that followed I was bombarded with text message from an unknown number calling me a bully, a dog snatcher and many other nasty and cruel names accompanied by vicious threats of what would happen to me if I ever tried to go near Becky or Ralph again. Although the number had been blocked, it was clear these messages were from the same angry individual who arrived at my front door some weeks earlier. I was horrified, frightened and I was utterly confused.

It took me a while to get my head around it all, to figure out why an unknown man, who was the new boyfriend of Becky, my narcissistic ex, would want to intimidate, harass and threaten me in such a way. Then I remembered who I was dealing with; Becky – an astute manipulator who could engage in the victim mode to suit her own needs at the drop of a hat. Not content at putting me through four years of toxic abuse, not even satisfied that she had taken my bloody dog from me, but she was now, for some unknown reason, putting me through the torture of living under threat from her new boyfriend. I can only imagine the bullshit string of lies she made up. Crying to him about how she had naively walked past my house with Ralph that day heading to the park, and how I must have seen them from the living room window, rushed out through the front door, scaled the fence and attempted to grab the dog from her tiny little innocent hands. How she held onto the lead for dear life, not wanting her poor, beloved Ralph to be captured by this cruel and mean ex of hers. All this would have been told through a captivating performance of tears and snotters to emphasise her anguish at the ordeal she had encountered. This man, this newfound *supply* of Becky's the whole time being manipulated and aroused into protective mode by her story, anger growing inside him at the thought of me harming his beloved girlfriend.

I have no doubt that she goaded him, relentlessly playing the victim and stirring up his anger and hatred towards me to make herself feel good. She was obviously in the early stages of her new relationship with this man, and so she was priming him and moulding him into her loyal and protective partner and part of that was creating a situation of two against one. She managed to turn a complete and utter stranger, someone who I had never met, never even spoken to, against me with such vengeance and hatred through her manipulation. She had succeeded in her attempt to make me suffer, to make me feel fear and panic while making herself feel loved, protected and looked after by her latest victim. There is a lesson to be learnt here; a narcissist has a sick mind that willingly and purposefully plays dangerous games with those it captures. Be careful whose team you join.

CHAPTER 12

POST SEPARATION ABUSE

It's fair to say that anyone who has fallen victim to a narcissist and their manipulative psychological abuse often believes that the hardest part is leaving. Sadly, ending these toxic relationships is unfortunately not the end of your suffering. It's just the end of part 1 and the beginning of part 2 – the post separation abuse.

You have finally seen the narc for what he or she is and taken the bold and brave steps needed to end your dangerously volatile relationship. The narc is no longer the driver, the decision maker, the puppeteer and this lack of control puts them in a very uncomfortable position.

A narcissist will feel very vulnerable when they are not dominating the relationship and in order to regain their feeling of superiority and control, they may do one of two things as they attempt to resuscitate their supply. They will either:

- Adopt a charm offensive campaign towards the victim of love bombing to bring them back under their influence under the guise that they have changed.

- Ramp up the abuse overtly to assert their feeling of control over the victim using such things as finances and children to intimidate and create fear in the victim, coercively controlling them onto thinking they can't possibly leave the relationship.

The charm offensive, or Hoovering as it's often referred to by therapists, is when the narc attempts to convince you that they have changed. This may be presented as loving and sentimental messages, presenting themselves in a calm and respectful manner or showering you with attention and complements. They often appear heartbroken over losing you and will appear to be taking responsibly while profusely apologising for their behaviours and promising to change their ways. They may even create a sudden 'crisis' and you are the only person they can turn to. This performance is another manipulative tactic used by the narc as they attempt to influence your emotions and hoover you back in. None of this is real and there isn't even an ounce of sincerity in their apology. It's important you understand that this is nothing more than an award-winning performance and well thought out self-scripted lip service. If they were really a nice, genuine, loving and respectful partner then neither of you would be in this situation in the first place.

If the charm offense tactic is not the narc's preferred method, or perhaps they attempted it but quickly realised you were not to be fooled, then the second option and probably the worst one is deployed…. ramping up the abuse.

Each situation and relationship are obviously different and the dynamics of finances, children, property, businesses etc. will all become factors in how the narc will carry out their persistent and deliberate acts of control, manipulation and abuse in order to weaken, hurt and frighten you. They want to govern you; they NEED to have you in their life in order to maintain their narcissistic supply and they will go to any lengths to get what they want. They cause as much damage to you mentally, financially, emotionally and psychologically as they can. Remember, the weaker their victim becomes - the stronger they feel.

'RUTH'

THE KING AND HIS CASTLE

I always knew that it was going to be hard to end my marriage. It had taken me 14 years to figure out that my husband and father to my 3 children was a covert narcissist. I didn't want to see it. I wanted my marriage to work and as a result had spent those years suppressing his countless painful words and behaviours. I was heartbroken to the point that I had no choice but to admit to myself that I was in an abusive marriage, and I needed to get out. I was painfully aware that leaving him was going to have its challenges. To some it may appear a pretty straightforward exercise - if you aren't happy in your marriage then leave, find a solicitor and file for divorce. That might work out fine when you are dealing with a normal person, but unless you have experienced a narcissistic relationship for yourself, it is very hard to explain the extent their toxic manipulation can go to.

His reaction to the Solicitors letter which arrived in the post that Saturday morning stating that I was filing for divorce and my intentions to apply for full custody of the children was one of silence. After reading it quietly with an emotionless expression on his face he simply folded the letter back up along its neatly creased lines and placed it back into its envelope before setting it down on the kitchen bench and simply saying,
"So that's the way you want to play it?"

From his stoic demeanour and the impassive tone in his voice I could tell it was a statement rather than a question to which he was requiring a response.

Needless to say, the letter arriving was not exactly a surprise to him. I had been threatening to end the marriage for some months and he knew I was serious. I had made it clear that starting again, rebuilding things and trying to get me back was never going to be an option. It was over and I explicitly told him that I would never be able to forgive and forget the years of lying and cheating, the twisted arguments and blame shifting, the endless guilt trips and countless put downs and I certainly wasn't about to fall foul to any type of fake apologies and empty promises of change. He would need a total personality replacement for that and last time I checked those weren't available on the NHS!

I obviously had a pretty good idea of what he had been capable of while I was in the relationship but the words 'you ain't seen nothing yet' ring very true when you try to leave...trust me.

His first move the very next morning was to remove the fuel card from my purse. He ran a transport company and so fuel cards were used by both of us and were funded directly from the business. As a housewife I had very little income bar the housekeeping money he lodged into the joint account at the beginning of the month. Without the fuel card I would need to use the money which was earmarked for the groceries, school dinners and the usual bits and bobs needed for the kids. I probably used around £200 worth of fuel each month, so this was going to result in us choosing to either eat or get from A to B. Of course I confronted him about this.

"How am I supposed to get the kids to and from school if I don't have the money to put fuel in the car?" I asked

"The school is only two miles away. You've all got legs, haven't you? WALK" was his simple response.

"And how would you like me to get the groceries in? I suppose you want me to walk the 18-mile round trip to Tesco and back lugging several shopping bags too, do you?"

He didn't respond to that question, instead he got up and coming as close to my face as he could he looked me coldly in the eye and said,

178

"I'm not leaving this house honey so if you want a divorce, you may start learning to stand on your own two feet."

For the next couple of days, he walked about with a smug expression on his face, totally unfazed by the situation he had created. He bought his own food, cooked his own dinners, he even bought washing powder and somehow managed to operate the washing machine of the first time in our married life. Of course, only washing his own clothes. Meanwhile I was growing more and more frustrated and my fears of struggling to cope with it all were getting worse. Of course this was his intention. He was exerting his power in order to get me to submit, to call off the divorce, paint that false smile upon my face that I'd been so accustomed to wearing and get back to being the dutiful housewife.

I was resilient to his bullying. I contacted my mum and asked her to lend me some money and for the next few days life carried on as normal – well normal isn't exactly how you would describe living with a narcissist, but I was able to fuel the car with the cash mum had lent me and had intended to put the rest towards buying groceries. A few days after borrowing the money from my mum, I went to the ATM to withdraw the regular housekeeping money from the joint account only to discover that he had beaten me to it. He had withdrawn every last penny.

Just when I thought I'd seen the worst of him over the years, that he couldn't possibly stoop any lower than he had already, here he was literally taking the food from our mouths. It was in that moment I realised just what a nasty, wicked, selfish human being I was dealing with. He was trying to make me feel helpless, attempting to back me into a corner where I would have nowhere to go but back to him. I wasn't going to let that happen!

How could he do that? How could he be so cruel as to take the very food from the mouths of his own children?

You would think by this stage very little would shock me about his behaviours, but I can tell you something I've learnt first-hand – a narc will do the unthinkable to get what they want and feel powerful. They act with no empathy or consideration for anyone, and I mean ANYONE other than themselves.

After he left for work the next morning I made the bold decision to phone a locksmith and, spending the last few quid I had to my name, I instructed him to change all the locks in the house. I wanted him out of my life, so I took matters into my own hands.

You can only imagine his reaction when he tried to get in later that evening! I had never been more grateful to have neighbours because there was no way he was going to draw attention to himself over the fact that I had kicked him out by causing a scene. So, his expected rage and aggression at not being able to get into the house was suppressed to save face. For the first time I was actually thankful that he was so protective of his image otherwise there would have been one almighty explosion that night!

I would love to be able to tell you that my bold and self-assured move had taught him a lesson and that he retreated into his shell and left me and the kids alone after this but unfortunately that was not the case.

Within hours of him leaving the property my phone was alight with text messages, mainly screen shots from Google searches he had conducted. Each one stating the law when it came to removing a partner from a house that you both jointly own. He wasted no time in telling me that he had as much right to be in the house as I did and if I did not give him a key and allow him back in then he would have no choice but to force entry. These raging, threatening text messages continued into the early hours of the morning. I got very little sleep as you can imagine, and he had succeeded in making me fearful. He was angry now and I knew only too well where his anger could lead.

The next morning couldn't come soon enough and at 9am I was straight onto the phone with my Solicitor. I was hoping beyond all hope that he would give me something, anything to keep this man away from me, the kids and the house. I emailed him screenshots of his nasty text messages threatening to gain entry to the house and explained how frightened I was. I couldn't believe it when my solicitor sympathetically told me that I was powerless, and the narc did in fact have as much right to be in the property as me and the kids did. Unless I obtained a Non-Molestation Order or a Restraining Order from the Courts, he was unable to help me. To obtain either of these Orders I would need to report the incident to the police. However, my Solicitor went on to inform me that because his conduct had been made via telephone and he had not physically assaulted me the likelihood of getting one or the other was beyond slim. I was devastated. I actually couldn't believe what I was hearing. Basically, what I was being told was that if the narc had slapped me in the face I would have had a much better chance of getting a Non-Molestation Order. However, because his abuse was psychological and over property that we both owned, and therefore both had a legal right to be in, this was a civil matter and the police wouldn't get involved. Crazy!!

I was exhausted. Both emotionally and mentally not to mention completely and utterly lost as to what to do next. Making matters worse the narc was lighting up my phone again…. relentlessly. I received everything from threats that he was going to drill the locks on the doors and enter while I was sleeping to messages that he was going to bounce the mortgage and the house would be repossessed. It got so bad that I had to ask my neighbour to collect the kids from school because I was so fearful that the minute I left the property he would arrive with his toolkit, make entry and be inside the house waiting for me.

The feeling of hopelessness was almost paralyzing to the point that I very nearly considered giving up. All I wanted was to be free; to get out of this toxic marriage and away from the sole cause of all my misery, but it seemed impossible to see how I was going to manage. He could have his castle if that's what he wanted so much. I didn't care anymore; I just wanted out.

I swallowed what was left of my pride, broke down and confided in my mum and dad about everything. The years of abuse, the cheating, the humiliating way in which he would put me down in front of other people and of course the gruesome details of the recent events since he had received the Divorce notification. My mum was visibly upset and my dad, well my dad acted like the true and proper father that he

184

is. Together they somehow managed to convince me that I had enough strength to get through this to the end and that they would of course be beside me every step of the way. Within hours my dad was on the phone to estate agents seeking out any potential properties to rent. They would have loved for me and the kids to have moved in with them, but the practicalities of school and clubs meant that it wasn't an option. Plus, if I was going to do this right then I needed to stand on my own two feet even if that meant relying on their temporary financial help to do it.

We found a house locally that was affordable and convenient for school and within hours my mum was busy packing as much of mine and the kids belongings as she could. They were amazing. No, they were better than amazing…they were my saviours that day because without them I'm not sure I would have found the strength to continue with the fight.

My ex wanted to break me and if I'm honest, he very nearly did. He thought that by taking the fuel card and ultimately my only form of transport, removing all the money from the joint bank account and leaving me penniless, by threatening to have our house – the kid's home - repossessed that he would stop me leaving the utterly toxic, soul-destroying marriage. But he didn't win in the end.

Fast forward 18 months and me and the kids are well settled into our new home. I got a job at the local supermarket with great hours that work around school drop offs and pickups. I was also able to apply for some single parent benefits. After a long 4-month battle with the Child Maintenance Service trying to obtain details of his earning, my ex now also has to pay me a monthly sum so no more empty bank accounts! All in all, life is good. I would say I'm still recovering but my self-esteem has greatly improved, and I actually feel happy, which is a feeling that had been alien to me for so long. I'm attending a counsellor who specialises in Narcissistic Abuse twice a month which I know is really helping me come to terms with everything. She has provided me with so much insight into narcissism and helped me understand that financial control is in fact a form of abuse, which I was unaware of before. Unfortunately, it's commonly used by narcissists to gain power and control over their victims but sadly not much of it is ever heard or seen. I hope this story highlights this form of control and maybe we should all keep a separate bank account in our own name…just in case.

CHAPTER 13

D.I.V.O.R.C.E

Being married to and subsequently divorcing any sort of narcissist can be gruelling to say the least however, I honestly believe that the rich narc is in a league of his or her own. Their financial status can be used as a powerful tool in their arsenal of weapons especially when it comes to legal battles. They can afford to employ the best solicitors and barristers and of course they are in no rush to hurry proceedings along. In fact, the narc will often deliberately create delays by;

* Ignoring correspondence from the victim's solicitor
 *Delaying handing over relevant documents
* Making up fabricated stories which puts the victim in a position of having to defend themselves
* Not turning up or cancelling arranged court dates or counsel meetings

These are just a few of the tactics used by the narc to create emotional distress, immense frustration and of course increased legal fees which have very little impact on the rich narc's healthy bank balance.

These tactical games are intentional and aimed to directly provoke and intimidate the victim as they attempt to stand up to and expose the narcissist for what they are. These unnecessary delays in turn generate a massive financial burden on the victim, which again is something the narc will take great pleasure from creating.

In many cases the narc does not usually want a divorce and is quite happy to plod along playing these vindictive and infuriating games for as long as they possibly can. Remember, to them you are their supply and they don't want that supply to end so will endeavour to put as many barriers in your way when it comes to you attempting to cut ties with them.

While these tactics are used by the narc in an attempt to prolong their supply, in an unfair twist they also provide them with yet even more attention. You are now under their control. You are requesting, albeit through your legal team, something from them and they thrive on this attention. You require their cooperation in order to ultimately achieve your goal which is a divorce and to cut them out of your life for good. This goes against the very being of the narc, so their cooperation is not something they are going to give easily.

A little bit of legal education here for you as I put my Erin Brockovich hat on.

Divorce in Northern Ireland can be granted on only 5 terms:
**Grounds for Divorce may differ depending on the country.

- **Adultery** - which can be very hard to prove
- **Desertion** - when one party takes themselves off and acts as if they don't have a spouse
- **Unreasonable Behaviour** – covers a multitude of issues
- **2 years separated with consent of the other spouse** - this is when both parties have lived apart for 2 years or more and are both in agreement of a divorce
- **5 years separated without consent of the other spouse** - this is when both parties have lived apart for 5 years or more and the consent of the other spouse is not required to proceed with a divorce

Now, it will perhaps be a shock to learn that the grounds of Unreasonable Behaviour can cover a multitude of things. The scope is anything from excessive drinking to leaving your socks on the floor! The Court is not there to decide what is deemed to be unreasonable within a marriage as this is personal and can greatly differ from one marriage to the next. One party for example might be agreeable to their partner joining a religious cult while in another marriage this would not be seen as reasonable behaviour and so grounds for divorce are present.

Due to the limited grounds on offer for divorce, even though the Unreasonable Behaviour covers a
multitude of reasons, couples who simply fall out of love with each other and have no grounds against each other to proceed would therefore opt for the 2 years separated option and must live apart for 2 years before they can apply to the Courts for a divorce.

Now, in dealing with a narc you will more than likely come across adultery within the marriage, but like I've said already this is a very hard one to prove and will potentially involve other individuals who will be called to give evidence at a hearing. The divorce is no longer a straightforward sitting in front of the Judge for 20 mins to get the paperwork stamped, as it can turn into a prolonged and lengthy case.
For this reason, most people seeking a divorce from a narcissistic partner will do so on the grounds of Unreasonable Behaviour.

As with any of the grounds listed above, when an individual applies for a divorce, they become the 'Petitioner' and the other party will become the 'Respondent' and just as these titles suggest, the Petitioner will serve the Divorce Papers via their solicitor on the Respondent and await their response.

Now, over the past 24 months I have spoken to a lot of survivors of narcissistic abuse, and many were unfortunately tied up in toxic marriages and inevitably had to travel down the divorce route. In every single case each victim had initiated divorce proceedings using 'Unreasonable Behaviour' as their grounds. Guess what? Not one of the narcissistic partners signed the papers.

In each case, the narc contested the divorce. In layman's terms this means that the narc would not accept responsibility for the breakdown of the marriage and would not admit to any of the claims that were made against them in the divorce application.

In these instances, the narc 'Respondent' therefore needed to file a response to the divorce papers within 30 days of them being served, as 'Defended'. Then, within a further 28 days they would need to send an 'Answer to Divorce' form which would state why they disagreed with the Divorce.

In all the cases I have been privy too, every single one of the narcissistic partners denied any wrongdoing within the marriage and claimed the allegations made against them, sighted within the divorce papers were nothing more than fabricated lies. This is not surprising when you consider that the typical character traits of a narcissist would be to deny any responsibility for their dysfunctional behaviours, refuse to accept accountability and of course shift the blame onto their victim.

However, their refusal to accept responsibility for the breakdown of their marriage creates an even harder, drawn out and often tactical and unfair playing field as you are now dealing with a *Contested Divorce.*

A Contested Divorce in summary is a divorce where the two parties cannot come to an agreement on the terms of the divorce.

Put simply; the victim wants to divorce the narcissist on the grounds of Unreasonable Behaviour, however the narcissist will not accept that his or her behaviour was unreasonable and therefore refuses to sign the divorce papers issued to them. The last thing a narcissist wants to see is a divorce being granted and a certificate issued which states their name and their behaviours as the reason for why the marriage has ended. Remember - blame is not something they are willing to accept.

It is also quite common for the narcissist to complicate matters further by shifting the blame onto the victim, making false claims and alleging that it was the victim's behaviours which ultimately caused the breakdown of the marriage.

Due to the apparent conflict in stories between both parties, much more paperwork is required as the legal teams attempt to ascertain blame or at the very least a compromise from one or other party to enable them to conclude the divorce. Obviously more paperwork means more money which, as I've said above, isn't an issue to a wealthy narc but to the victim can be a heavy burden. This explains why many victims at this stage may opt to just accept responsibility, albeit a false confession, as they see it as their only option to get a divorce finalised without the rising costs and further drawn-out dramas.

However, one such victim felt the battle of a Contested Divorce was worth every penny of her hard-earned cash. She was the victim of many years of narcissistic abuse and there was no way she was going to passively accept the blame shifting. Not this time.

'CAROLINE'

I'LL SEE YOU IN COURT

I had applied for a divorce from Phil, my narcissistic husband following 10 years of abuse. After a lengthy meeting with my Solicitor the application was filed on the grounds of 'Unreasonable Behaviour'. I could have applied for the divorce on the grounds of adultery, but my solicitor advised that it would be easier and much more straightforward to use the Unreasonable Behaviour option. As predicted, he contested the divorce, claimed his innocence in all aspects of my allegations against him and in an unprecedented twist proceeded with serving his own divorce papers on me for *my* Unreasonable Behaviour. If you didn't laugh, you'd cry!

Needless to say, the petition he served on me claiming my alleged Unreasonable Behaviour was nothing short of a Jackanory script of lies and make-believe, but when you've dealt with a narc for as long as I have you soon come to learn that lies are second nature to them.

Now, I should add at this point that one important fact of a divorce is that the costs lie with the party at fault......so whoever gets granted the divorce will have their legal bills paid by the other party. This decision is ultimately up to the Judge who reviews all the relevant information and statements, etc. and comes to his final conclusion.

Anyway, due to Phil's inability to admit responsibility, we were now dealing with a Contested Divorce and therefore the case was greatly delayed for obvious reasons. A lot more legal to-ing and fro-ing was created between my solicitor and his and then of course there was the added expenses from the

Barrister who was required to write and submit several additional reports and documents to the court.

I would have literally bet my last penny that this was something Phil was over the moon about. It meant he was back in control again, twisting the truth and fabricating stories that would ultimately delay the final outcome for which he knew now I was desperate to achieve to get him out of my life.

I have no doubt that in his deluded state of mind Phil thought he would be able to convince legal teams that he was in fact the long-suffering victim in the marriage and that I, under immense mental and financial stress would bow out, taking responsibility for the breakdown of the relationship as the heat got too much to handle. I imagine he was like a dog with two tails during this whole sordid and unnecessary battle because that's how narcs get their kicks…...breaking people down. Well, he might have bent me from time to time, but I was never going to break!

A very frustrating 2 years passed by…yes, along with a helping hand from Covid, the Court's annual summer holidays and of course all the unnecessary delays he created, it took two full years for us to eventually get into Court. Just to put this into perspective, normally the whole process of getting a divorce usually takes around 5 months but that is when both parties act in a timely manner and don't attempt to block or delay any part of the otherwise straightforward process.

So, there we were in front of the Judge who instead of having a single divorce application signed by both parties, now had two applications for divorce in front of him each claiming that they were the wronged party.

Now, you don't need me to tell you that Judges are not only highly intelligent individuals, but they are also very, very well experienced and as a Divorce Judge they would have seen countless cases of pointing the finger and blame shifting going on which would naturally make it very hard to see the truth among the lies.

My case however was presented to the Judge with a little bit of extra evidence which Phil failed to realise the importance of. I cannot emphasise enough how important it is to keep meticulous records of everything when you are in a relationship with a narcissist – you never know when you might need them. As the saying goes, 'You'd rather be looking at it than looking for it'

You see the Divorce Court wasn't the only Court Phil and I had found ourselves attending. During the whole separation proceedings, we attended Family Court as, not surprisingly we were unable to come to a satisfactory arrangement around child contact with our two daughters. He wanted full custody, which of course there wasn't a cat's chance in hell I was going to give him. He was seriously deluded to even think he could cope with the children considering he never spent any time with them, but a narcissist will often become *Parent of the Year* if they think they can take something from you that you never want to give up. It was just another game to him, another form of coercive control.

" You do as I say or I'll abuse my parental rights in court and take the kids off you!"

This was a regular threat I'd heard ever since we had separated. At the beginning these threats had caused me great anxiety and worry but then I soon realised that was his plan. He wanted to make me fearful that I could lose my children and therefore I would agree to his crazy demands around contact. I had come to know him and his manipulation very well, so I took matters into my own hands and prevented contact with the kids for a fortnight. During this time Phil swiftly made an application to Family Court for access. Interestingly enough, it was not for the full custody which he had so often threatened me with but just a few nights a week and every other weekend. I suspected his solicitor had managed to somehow convince him that it would only be in exceptional circumstances that the Judge would grant full custody to one or other parent.

Anyway, during the initial Court hearing I had produced some very damning evidence against Phil which I had managed to record and keep. It was a rather nasty verbally abusive rant in which he had called me every name under the sun, told me to die of cancer and made several threats to 'ruin me'. Sadly, these were all things I had gotten used to hearing, but on this occasion, I decided to use my mobile phone to record the unpleasant event. This new piece of evidence was presented in Court much to the dismay of Phil's legal team. They tried to get it thrown out by claiming it had been covertly obtained. The Judge said he would listen to the recording in his Chambers and make the decision based on its content whether it was relevant to the case.

I will never forget the Judge's facial expression as he returned to face us in Court after listening to that recording in his chambers. To say he was disgusted was an understatement and he verbalised this directly to Phil calling it "…a despicable and deplorable act".

The recording had certainly highlighted to the Court Phil's shockingly aggressive temper. However, what gave them real concern was the fact that the kids were audible in the background, evidencing that Phil had carried out this cruel and bullish rant in front of the girls.

Not only did the Judge grant his permission for the recording to be used as evidence, but he also called for a Fact-Finding Hearing.

This is a type of court hearing which allows a judge to consider if allegations of domestic abuse have taken place or not.

After a lengthy hearing spanning over four months and involving many witnesses, the Judge found Phil responsible for three counts of Domestic Abuse.

Despite these findings from Family Court, Phil still went on to contest my divorce application and continued with his attempts at painting me out to be the abuser and him nothing more than a poor, vulnerable victim. Perhaps he thought the two separate Courts would not share information or outcomes, or perhaps it was just a case that he believed his own lies so much that the actual evidence and factual findings were irrelevant to him.

Still, despite these Findings of Facts of Domestic Abuse from Family Court, he still maintained his status quo and approached the Divorce Courts with an 'I'm whiter than white' attitude and proceeded to attempt to convince a different Judge in a separate Court that he was not in fact an unreasonable individual and it was me who was to blame for the breakdown of the marriage.

Finally, our Court date had arrived and although the whole ordeal leading up to this day was long and arduous, justice prevailed in the end.

Speaking sternly to the Barrister representing Phil, it was apparent that the Honourable Mr Justice had thoroughly read through all the supporting reports and documents which had been presented to him by both Solicitors, including those from Family Court. He seemed almost irritated by the fact that Phil's Barrister had not been able to convince her client of what the inevitable outcome of this case was going to be, and seemed somewhat perplexed that they had therefore not withdrawn their application for Divorce prior to the court date. After offering a few words of sympathy for what I had obviously endured during the marriage and thereafter, and without hesitation he granted the divorce in my favour on the grounds of Unreasonable Behaviour. Phil's application against me was subsequently withdrawn and the icing on the cake…...all legal costs which now equated to approx. £12,000 were placed on Phil as the losing party.

Thursday 28th September 2023 will forever be the day I won my war.

CHAPTER 14

THE AFTERMATH

To assume that someone will experience narcissistic abuse and come out the other end unscathed is probably one of the biggest mistakes you will make.... right next to getting involved with one in the first place.

When someone has been at the receiving end of narcissistic abuse, it's fair to say they have gone through a significant ordeal. Although the abuse can reach various levels depending on the individual and of course the circumstances in which they are involved with the narc, the outcome will still be the same – the victim will have suffered significant trauma.
This trauma can be psychological, emotional and even sometimes physical.

Victims of narcissistic abuse have been lied to, cheated on, humiliated, insulted, manipulated, blackmailed, physically harmed and coerced. They are often left with very low self-esteem, depression and anxiety. They struggle to regulate their emotions and possess an intense feeling of unhappiness. These symptoms have been caused over a long period of time and are often deep rooted by the time they manage to escape from the power and control of the narcissist.

The trauma bestowed upon a victim of narcissistic abuse can cause them to suffer from *Hyperarousal*. (Sometimes referred to as *Hypervigilance*). Although Hyperarousal is a state of mind, it manifests itself through the human body causing those individuals to remain in a state of high alert and display many traits of anxiety. This may manifest as sleep disturbances, nightmares, muscle spasms, being easily startled, constantly aware of their environments, fears of reoccurrence, holding themselves in a state of tension, having an inability to concentrate or focus and generally being more irritable and angrier than they normally would be.

When we think about how insidious narcissistic abuse is and how the victims suffer chronic stress for many years, often living day to day in a fight or flight mode, it's easy to understand how they may develop hyperarousal symptoms. The body and mind have been in a constant state of arousal throughout the relationship and that sensation often increases during the period of post-separation until such times as the victim is able to finally go No Contact and begin their healing journey.

It is also recognised that mental and emotional trauma can manifest as pain throughout the body and people who have suffered from narcissistic abuse are more likely to experience chronic pain due to the connection between the mind and body. Many Institutes and Clinics have carried out in-depth research into this and their findings show that a much higher percentage of people with chronic pain report to have had trauma at some stage of their lives.

The trauma experienced does not necessarily have to be life-threatening situations but even events that overwhelm the body's natural ability to cope will cause the body to react. The nervous system becomes overactive, sensitive and overprotective causing the body to be stuck on high alert. Continued stress from being in a narcissistic relationship plays a massive role within our bodies and can worsen pain, increase inflammation, cause muscle tension, severe headaches, and skin issues but to name a few.

However, it's good to know that many of these symptoms are treatable and as the victim begins to heal from the trauma, symptoms do usually improve and in many cases can eventually disappear altogether. Nonetheless it does take time and being patient with oneself is crucial.

'JULIA'

<u>UNSEEN WOUNDS</u>

For me the post separation abuse lasted 4 years and within that time I was most definitely in fight mode. I had no other choice; I had two jobs to maintain, two kids to look after and life needed to keep going as normally as possible for their sake. However, on the outside I might have looked like I was coping in a methodical way but inside my body was manifesting the stresses beyond breaking point.

In 2020 I started getting very unusual symptoms which seemed to appear for no apparent reason. My legs would tingle and cramp at night-time causing restlessness and preventing me from getting a full night's sleep. My hands would go numb, headaches were a daily occurrence and pains, pains everywhere. My eyes would get sore and water like a river for no apparent reason. My hip would hurt, and I would experience such an overwhelming burning sensation that made me feel as if my lower back was on fire.

The strange thing was, all these symptoms came and went without any apparent reason and by the time I had gotten used to one particular pain or symptom, it would settle down again only for another one to appear in a different area of my body. This went on for months and months. As you might imagine, my sleep and my mood were being greatly affected making it nearly impossible to get through a full day's work without extreme fatigue and irritability taking over.
After some time, and with a bit of pressure from work, I made an appointment to see my GP.

After a lengthy appointment describing all my various symptoms and pains and the GP giving me a thorough examination, he delivered the news that he suspected I could have MS. As you might imagine, hearing that possible dragonise was extremely alarming and worrying.
Thankfully, the GP referred me onto Neurology who acted very quickly, and I was brought into hospital for MRI scans of my brain, neck and back within just a few days.
I can't begin to tell you how anxious I was. I couldn't stop thinking about everything I'd been though with my narcissistic ex-husband and the immense levels of stress he

had put me under. How bitterly unfair life would be if now, after coming through the most challenging years of my life I was to be diagnosed with a life changing illness like MS. Thankfully, I need not have worried as the results came back quickly and they were all clear. I did not have MS.

So, what was wrong with me then? What was the cause of my daily pains and changing symptoms? Seeming to not have any immediate answers for me, the GP prescribed me with Amitripyline. He explained that although this was a medication once used to treat depression, it was also prescribed to treat chronic pain, anxiety and insomnia.

Roll on another two years and the weird and unexplained symptoms kept coming. Night sweats, weight gain, thinning hair, joint pain…. you name it and I seemed to get it. Each aliment would come and after a few weeks or months would disappear again as quickly as they arrived. In 2022 I returned to my GP at this point completely and utterly pissed off with living like I was 80 years old.
I sat in his consulting room again trying to find the words to explain the latest bout of painful symptoms. He listened

quietly and once I had finished rhyming off everything, he just looked at me, tilted his head slightly and said.

"You've been through a lot, haven't you?"

As soon as he said it, I could feel the lump forming in my throat. You see due to the various visits I'd had to the GP surgery with the children over the past few years, this kind and knowledgeable doctor had an insight into the state of my psychologically abusive marriage and the torturous life I had been living at that time. I remember one particular visit, whilst in the midst of my toxic marriage, when I had the difficult task of trying to explain to him why my then 8-year-old daughter was wetting the bed. No make-believe story or farfetched lie was going to cut it. He was a doctor, and doctors are smart people, so I told him the truth. Abigail had been wetting the bed because she had been frightened of her Daddy, my husband. He used to get so mad when the kids got out of bed late at night and he would shout so much that the poor girl had become too afraid to creep to the bathroom in the middle of the night in case it alerted him, and the fearsome yelling would begin. Of course, there were no pills the GP could prescribe an eight-year-old for what was clearly anxiety but he did refer her to CALMS for counselling. Those sessions seemed to give Abigail a bit of reassurance. However, I do recall she never took a drink after 6pm ever again. This was something which was obviously advised by the counsellor in an attempt to ease her anxiety, knowing it would more than likely reduce the chance of her needing the toilet during the night.

That day, sitting in the GP's surgery with Abigail had been hard but, in some way, letting someone know what was going on at home, gave me an immediate sense of relief. It was something I have never done before, but I felt safe confiding in him. Of course, he had offered me leaflets and information on domestic abuse and various helplines I could avail of for support, but they were all regrettably placed in the bin outside the Surgery as we left. I wasn't ready to make that step just yet.

Now, a few years later and thankfully free from that toxic relationship, here I was sitting in his consultation room yet again about my mysterious pains.

"Well....what's that got to do with anything" I said defensively.

Don't go there I kept thinking.... don't look at me with that sympathetic head tilt and expectant eyes wanting me to break down and admit that I was drained. I was tired. I was worn out and exhausted to my very core. I was done.

I knew only too well what a hard and arduous road I had travelled over the past few years. I'd been holding in so many savage and raw emotions in an attempt to put on the brave face and get on with things for the sake of my kids and for my own sanity, refusing to give in and let the bastard break me! I'd been strong for too long and now that the relationship was over and the post separation abuse had been put to an end, it was almost as if my body was telling me that I could let go of it all now; the hurt, the anger, the heartbreak, the confusion, the fear, the stress. It felt like each suppressed emotion was piled up on top of each other like a mountain of rotting, rancid smelling rubbish waiting to be taken out so that I could finally be free of the heavy burden it held within me. But I was afraid. I was afraid of letting go and breaking down in case I was unable to get back up again. These emotions I held inside were almost like my prisoners of war and releasing them had unknown consequences. Add to that the guilt of self-sabotage I felt due to the numerous times I blamed myself for giving chance after chance. The trauma had been building up inside of me throughout the painful eight years of marriage to a narcissist and four years of fighting my way through a bitter divorce. To let all these savage emotions go and imagine that I could live my life in peace without fear, without worry, without stress was unthinkable.

"I'm here about my pains." I said in earnest response, trying to steer him back onto the path of least resistance.

He continued with conviction.
"I think the pains and symptoms you are experiencing are a direct result of what you have been through. Your past toxic relationship has without doubt caused you some significant trauma. Have you ever heard of a condition called Fibromyalgia?"
He was now looking at me a way that was both sympathetic and observant. He could see what I thought was hidden. He was looking at me with an acute awareness of everything I'd

been trying to hide from the outside world for what seemed like forever.

He carried on speaking in the knowledge that I was now unable to answer verbally due to the lump that had readily appeared in my throat, but the tears that were now free flowing down my cheeks gave him all the answer he needed. "Many people who develop Fibromyalgia have been through some sort of trauma. I believe that is what is happening to you. I would like to refer you for some trauma counselling and I'm also going to prescribe some medication for PTSD which I think might help you"

So, there it was. The scars of the narc had been left deeper than I ever imagined possible. Here I was over the battle and out the other side only to discover that my body - mentally and physically had been left with long lasting side effects.

The trauma counselling helped as did the medication. It took time and a lot of patience with myself. Thankfully the counsellor I was appointed had some personal experience of narcissistic abuse so that really helped. I felt that my healing journey was kick started there and then as she understood exactly what I had gone through and how I was feeling. For the first time I didn't feel alone.

It's now early 2024 and although I still take a small dose of Amitripyline to help me get a restful night's sleep, the pains are minimal now as are the headaches. I have my smile back and with a little more time and self-belief I am entirely positive that I will no longer suffer from any of the symptoms of fibromyalgia caused by my narcissistic ex.

Stay strong,

stay focused,

stay hopeful.

The best view comes after the hardest climb.

DEAR READER.........

Dear Reader,

Firstly, I would like to thank you for taking the time to read this book. It has without doubt been a labour of love of mine for the entire two years I've been working on it, and at times something which I worried I might not be unable to complete.

Narcissistic abuse affected me in the most horrid ways. It left me broken, depressed and utterly confused about my place in this world. I was lonely and unhappy, fearful and ashamed, and just like many others, I often thought there was no way out.

Then, there was a day when something just clicked. I can't describe it any more than I can understand it, but from that day on everything for the first time was perfectly, untaintedly clear. I had been a victim of narcissistic abuse.

That is not always an easy thing to admit, let alone talk about. Those who have never been affected directly are unable to truly understand what you've gone through, nor can they comprehend the incredible levels of control and manipulation you have been living under.

The reason I want to tell you this is because if you are in a relationship with someone who makes you question your own mind, your self-worth and your value, then you need to reconsider your options.

I empathise with those who find themselves in a toxic, psychologically abusive relationship and understand how we lose every shred of hope, along with our confidence, self-esteem and inner strength. We struggle to find the courage it takes to leave or to remove the narcissistic person from our life and find it even harder to imagine how we could ever be free from the emotional entrapment they have built around us.

Sometimes we must get knocked down lower than we have ever been in order to stand up taller than we ever were. I want to tell you that everything can and will change. That change must start with you, but first you must believe in YOU.
You must remind yourself on a daily basis that you are worth more than how they make you feel. You are important, you are loved, and you are going to smile again…I promise.

Each and every one of us deserves genuine, authentic love and you, my dear reader, are no different. You are not required to put up with disrespect, disloyalty, rage, aggression and selfish control and that is exactly what you must keep reminding yourself of. You are worth so much more than what someone has unfortunately made you believe.

You deserve to find someone who understands that love is not a game, but rather that it is an investment. You deserve to be treated like a priority not an option. You deserve someone who respects your boundaries, who is willing to nurture your emotions and listen to your words. Ultimately, you deserve BETTER, and if BETTER hasn't knocked upon your door just yet then being in a relationship with yourself is often the perfect place to wait. After all, you do not need another person to make you feel validated – you are enough on your own.

It is my hope that this book has brought you comfort, understanding and an ability to make sense of, not only what narcissistic abuse is, but how it plays out in real life situations. I hope anyone who has suffered at the hands of a narcissistic individual knows they are not alone and can take comfort from the fact that your experience, as hard as it was, did not break you – only bent you temporarily.

Your journey has equipped you with an invisible coat of armour; you will never fall foul to a narcissist again. Your standards will be higher than ever before as you begin the next chapter of your life knowing that your self-worth is not based on the behaviours and opinions of another nor is it something you will ever compromise again.

It is never too late to find your true self and I sincerely hope that you gather the strength to do what you must. I wish you all a peaceful, happy and narc-free life where you are appreciated, respected and above all - loved for who you are.

Never doubt your worth.

Debbie x

BETTER DAYS ARE COMING...

WE ARE ALL BOOKS

Within us we hold our individual stories of life's journey.

Stories of love and romance,

of loss and regret,

of missed opportunities,

unimaginable heartache and unspeakable truths.

We all have a front cover for others to view,

giving them an opportunity to judge us,

with no real knowledge of

what might be held behind our indefinable exterior.

Each one of us is unique.

With others we may share a similar mind-set,

we may even share the same language,

skin colour or some of life's many struggles.

But still, we remain as individuals.

Each one of us longing to be lovingly held

in our admirer's hands and heart.

Hoping we are loyally preserved,

respected and accepted for what we are.

All of us holding a fear of rejection,

a sincere dread of being left on the shelf

to watch life's many possibilities, pass by

without a chance to experience them.

Dust gathering dust as we are sadly forgotten.

Some of us are created in simplicity

while others are here through

the heart-breaking struggles and determination of their author.

Some of us have learnt hard life lessons,

while some of us are still to travel those roads.

But no matter the hows or the whys,

regardless of which direction our words are strung together,

we unite within the pages of our individual book.

We are all books.

Deborah Louise Wheeler 2024

RESOURCES

Narcissistic abuse is a form of psychological and emotional abuse which can lead to anxiety, depression, low self-esteem, and other mental health issues such as post-traumatic stress disorder. If you feel like you need further guidance on how to deal with a narcissistic individual or support on how to cope with the effects their abuse has, then please reach out to any of the following resources:

RE.VIVE.COACHING

www.re-vive-coaching.co.uk

Email – info@re-vive-coaching.co.uk

WOMEN'S AID

www.womensaid.org.uk

Email – helpline@womensaid.org.uk

MENS ADVISORY PROJECT

www.mapni.co.uk

Telephone Belfast – 028 90241929

Telephone Foyle – 028 7116 0001

ANXIETY UK

www.anxietyuk.org.uk

Helpline – 03444 775 774

SHOUT

Email – info@giveusashout.org

Text – SHOUT to 85258

CITIZENS ADVICE BUREAU

www.citizensadvice.org.uk

ABOUT THE AUTHOR

This is the debut offering from Deborah Louise Wheeler, who draws on her own harrowing firsthand experiences to bring you this insightful look at narcissism and the effects it can have on others.

Originally from Moira, she now lives in the small village of Eglish in Co Tyrone, with her partner Keith and two daughters Tia and Brooke.

Deborah attended Forthill Girls High School in Lisburn before completing her education at Lisburn College from where she went on to begin her career in Banking. After nearly twelve years in Finance, Deborah took the plunge into self-employment where she went on to be the founder of **Queen Bee Naturals, Ink-Sential Professional Tattoo Care, Wild & Dandy** and most recently **RE.VIVE.COACHING** where she offers support and guidance to others who have been affected by narcissistic abuse.

When Deborah isn't busy working in her businesses, she can often be found relaxing at her gorgeous caravan on the stunning coast of Co Down with a couple of fur babies in tow!

If you would like to follow
Deborah on Social media
then please scan this QR code.

Thank you x